COMMERCIAL CYBER ESPIONAGE AND BARRIERS TO DIGITAL TRADE IN CHINA

HEARING

BEFORE THE

U.S.-CHINA ECONOMIC AND SECURITY REVIEW COMMISSION

ONE HUNDRED FOURTEENTH CONGRESS
FIRST SESSION

MONDAY, JUNE 15, 2015

Printed for use of the
United States-China Economic and Security Review Commission
Available via the World Wide Web: www.uscc.gov

UNITED STATES-CHINA ECONOMIC AND SECURITY REVIEW COMMISSION

WASHINGTON: 2015

U.S.-CHINA ECONOMIC AND SECURITY REVIEW COMMISSION

Hon. WILLIAM A. REINSCH, *Chairman*
Hon. DENNIS C. SHEA, *Vice Chairman*

Commissioners:

CAROLYN BARTHOLOMEW	DANIEL M. SLANE
PETER BROOKES	SEN. JAMES TALENT
ROBIN CLEVELAND	DR. KATHERINE C. TOBIN
JEFFREY L. FIEDLER	MICHAEL R. WESSEL
SEN. CARTE P. GOODWIN	DR. LARRY M. WORTZEL

MICHAEL R. DANIS, *Executive Director*

The Commission was created on October 30, 2000 by the Floyd D. Spence National Defense Authorization Act for 2001 § 1238, Public Law No. 106-398, 114 STAT. 1654A-334 (2000) (codified at 22 U.S.C. § 7002 (2001), as amended by the Treasury and General Government Appropriations Act for 2002 § 645 (regarding employment status of staff) & § 648 (regarding changing annual report due date from March to June), Public Law No. 107-67, 115 STAT. 514 (Nov. 12, 2001); as amended by Division P of the "Consolidated Appropriations Resolution, 2003," Pub L. No. 108-7 (Feb. 20, 2003) (regarding Commission name change, terms of Commissioners, and responsibilities of the Commission); as amended by Public Law No. 109-108 (H.R. 2862) (Nov. 22, 2005) (regarding responsibilities of Commission and applicability of FACA); as amended by Division J of the "Consolidated Appropriations Act, 2008," Public Law Nol. 110-161 (December 26, 2007) (regarding responsibilities of the Commission, and changing the Annual Report due date from June to December); as amended by the Carl Levin and Howard P. "Buck" McKeon National Defense Authorization Act for Fiscal Year 2015, P.L. 113-291 (December 19, 2014) (regarding responsibilities of the Commission).

The Commission's full charter is available at www.uscc.gov.

September 01, 2015

The Honorable Orrin Hatch
President Pro Tempore of the Senate, Washington, D.C. 20510
The Honorable John A. Boehner
Speaker of the House of Representatives, Washington, D.C. 20515

DEAR SENATOR HATCH AND SPEAKER BOEHNER:

We are pleased to notify you of the Commission's June 15, 2015 public hearing on "Commercial Cyber Espionage and Barriers to Digital Trade in China." The Floyd D. Spence National Defense Authorization Act (amended by Pub. L. No. 109-108, section 635(a) and amended by Pub. L. No. 113-291, Section 1259 B) provides the basis for this hearing.

At the hearing, the Commissioners received testimony from the following witnesses: Samm Sacks, China Analyst, Eurasia Group; Matthew Schruers, Vice President for Law & Policy, Computer & Communications Industry Association; Paul M. Tiao, Partner, Hunton & Williams; Dennis F. Poindexter, author of The Chinese Information War, Espionage, Cyberwar, Communications Control and Related Threats to United States Interests; and Jen Weedon, Manager, Threat Intelligence and Strategic Analysis, FireEye and Mandiant, Inc. The hearing examined China's use of standards, regulation, and censorship as a market-entry barrier. It also examined China's use of cyber espionage to gather information for commercial purposes, including turning over U.S. intellectual property to competing Chinese state-owned enterprises. Lastly, the Commission also heard expert witnesses address the OPM breach and related hacking of federal agencies.

We note that prepared statements for the hearing, the hearing transcript, and supporting documents submitted by the witnesses are available on the Commission's website at www.USCC.gov. Members and the staff of the Commission are available to provide more detailed briefings. We hope these materials will be helpful to the Congress as it continues its assessment of U.S.-China relations and their impact on U.S. security.

The Commission will examine in greater depth these issues, and the other issues enumerated in its statutory mandate, in its 2015 Annual Report that will be submitted to Congress in November 2015. Should you have any questions regarding this hearing or any other issue related to China, please do not hesitate to have your staff contact Communications Director and Congressional Liaison, Anthony Demarino, at (202) 624-1496 or via email at ADemarino@uscc.gov.

Sincerely yours,

Hon. William A. Reinsch
Chairman

Hon. Dennis C. Shea
Vice Chairman

CONTENTS

MONDAY, JUNE 15, 2015

COMMERCIAL CYBER ESPIONAGE AND BARRIERS TO DIGITAL TRADE IN CHINA

COMMERCIAL CYBER ESPIONAGE AND BARRIERS TO DIGITAL TRADE IN CHINA

MONDAY, JUNE 15, 2015

_____

U.S.-CHINA ECONOMIC AND SECURITY REVIEW COMMISSION

Washington, D.C.

The Commission met in Room 608 of the Dirksen Senate Office Building in Washington, DC at 9:00 a.m., Commissioner Carte P. Goodwin and Vice Chairman Dennis Shea (Hearing Co-Chairs), presiding.

OPENING STATEMENT OF VICE CHAIRMAN DENNIS C. SHEA
HEARING CO-CHAIR

VICE CHAIRMAN SHEA: Well, good morning, everyone, and thank you for being here today. Before I go any further, I'd like to thank Senate Budget Committee Chairman Mike Enzi for the use of this hearing room and also thank the staff of the Senate Budget Committee for helping make this possible.

This morning's hearing is the last of seven in our 2015 Annual Report cycle. We have an excellent line-up of witnesses on a very important and I must say timely topic. Our hearing today concerns cyber espionage and barriers to digital trade in China.

I thank the witnesses for their written testimony submitted in advance for the record and now posted on our Web site at uscc.gov.

Only two months ago President Obama declared a national emergency as a result of the quote, "increasing prevalence and severity of malicious cyber-enabled" attacks that "constitute an unusual and extraordinary threat to the national security, foreign policy, and economy of the United States."

And only two weeks ago the nation learned that an attack on the Office of Personnel Management resulted in the theft of the personal information of four million current and former federal workers and retirees. Especially worrisome is the fact that the attackers apparently obtained the records of federal workers who have received security clearances from the OPM, which conducts about 80 percent of the security investigations and clearances for the federal workforce.

This intrusion indicates a high degree of planning and sophistication. It followed a pattern that has become all too familiar: the use of zero-day malware that eluded commercial anti-spyware detection and servers or routing indicators located in China. And, of course, the standard denials from the government in Beijing that it does not conduct espionage on the United States because that would be illegal.

I would like to ask the panelists to please keep to our seven-minute rule, seven minutes to summarize your written testimony. This provides us the time for an in-depth question and answer period--and we're not bashful about asking questions--and for discussion and debate among the panelists.

Now, I would like to introduce my co-chair, Commissioner Carte Goodwin, who will also introduce the first panel.

OPENING STATEMENT OF COMMISSIONER CARTE P. GOODWIN
HEARING CO-CHAIR

HEARING CO-CHAIR GOODWIN: Thank you, Chairman Shea.

Our first panel today will examine a disturbing trend in which the Chinese government uses standards and regulations and even censorship to create regulatory barriers to U.S. tech companies seeking to enter the Chinese marketplace.

This propensity to use regulations as a means to diminish competition unfortunately is not new. Indeed, much of this Commission's time since its creation in 2001 has been spent studying and documenting the ways in which Chinese government seeks to attract foreign investment, especially from the United States, and then spends years favoring domestic companies over their U.S. counterparts while simultaneously refusing to protect intellectual property of U.S. companies from piracy and counterfeiting.

This, of course, is especially pronounced in the information and communications tech sector. Recently the government in Beijing has proposed a series of regulatory provisions that would require U.S. tech companies and their foreign customers, especially financial institutions and banks, to turn over source code and encryption software, effectively creating backdoor entry points into otherwise secure networks, all being done, of course, under the guise of cybersecurity.

PANEL I INTRODUCTION BY COMMISSIONER CARTE P. GOODWIN

HEARING CO-CHAIR GOODWIN: Our first panel today will focus on these recently proposed regulatory barriers to digital trade in China and the corresponding costs to U.S. firms.

We are pleased to welcome Samm Sacks to the panel, who's a China analyst at the Eurasia Group here their Washington office. Prior to joining the Eurasia Group, Ms. Sacks was an analyst at Booz Allen Hamilton and Defense Group, Inc., advising both government and corporate clients on Chinese science and technology development.

She has previously worked for the Office of the Secretary of Defense and was a Fulbright Scholar in Beijing.

Our second panelist is Matt Schruers of the Computer & Communications Industry Association where he is the Vice President for Law and Policy focusing on intellectual property, competition and trade. In his spare time, Mr. Schruers is also an adjunct professor of intellectual property at the Georgetown University Law Center and the Georgetown Graduate Program on communication, culture and technology.

Welcome to you both. Mr. Schruers.

OPENING STATEMENT OF MATTHEW SCHRUERS, VICE PRESIDENT FOR LAW & POLICY, COMPUTER & COMMUNICATIONS INDUSTRY ASSOCIATION

MR. SCHRUERS: Good morning. Thank you.

I appreciate the opportunity to speak with you today. My name is Matt Schruers with the Computer & Communications Industry Association, and I look forward to an opportunity to discuss barriers to digital trade in China.

CCIA if you don't know is a trade association of Internet and technology firms which has advocated for openness, fair trade, and competition for over 40 years.

And today my remarks are going to focus on barriers to trade in the form of filtering, censoring and blocking of Internet services, which is crucial to U.S. interests.

While Internet censorship is frequently discussed through the lens of human rights, restrictions on the free flow of information also have substantial economic consequences, and so what we're discussing is not just a values question but also a question of economic security.

The Internet's contribution to the U.S. economy today exceeds that of traditional industries like agriculture, arts, entertainment, recreation, construction, even the federal government itself, and the Internet is also one of the consistent bright spots and success stories when it comes to U.S. exports.

So in light of all this, a level playing field for Internet services should be a U.S. priority, but today the playing field is not at all level. Firms seeking to export services, as you have already mentioned, encounter numerous barriers in China, including obligations on intermediaries to block or disappear content or search results, the imposition of technology mandates, whether it is to build in a particular manner or to disclose information that either hobble user privacy or compromise security through the means of backdoors or blocking, filtering and censoring of services or platforms, which is executed at the network level through state control of telecommunications infrastructure.

At least three separate NGOs, the U.S. International Trade Commission, and reports by the USTR in the form of the National Trade Estimate have all extensively catalogued ongoing filtering, censoring, and blocking, which are pointed to more specifically in the written statement that I have provided.

And whether these techniques are, in fact, aimed at maintaining social control or a pretext for playing favorites with local firms, or some combination of both is really irrelevant to the question of whether or not these are barriers to trade. It's fairly clear that these are, in fact, unlawful in relation to Chinese international obligations. And the consequence of this is that U.S. firms have systematically been forced out of the Chinese market in recent years, even as their Chinese competitors are accessing the U.S. market to engage leading providers of financial services, legal services and technical services.

In fact, some of the largest IPOs in history have been Chinese firms raising capital on U.S. markets, using U.S. underwriters and other U.S. consultants and services. Western investors value these opportunities very highly because they know these companies have exclusive access to a market which is a growing opportunity and strategically key, where their U.S. competitors are hobbled or completely blocked.

Now, as an association that has championed open trade and competition for over 40 years, CCIA welcomes the emergence of Chinese firms in the Internet sector, but with global aspirations come global obligations, and that includes compliance with international norms, including those that pertain to WTO members.

Under the WTO, we have both the General Agreement on Tariffs and Trade, GATT, and the General Agreement on Trade in Services, under which a WTO participant must permit fair market access for goods and services, abide by principles of nondiscrimination and national treatment, and regulate in a transparent and predictable manner, which at least will allow for the possibility of judicial or administrative review and oversight of decisions that are trade related.

The online filtering and blocking that we see does not comply with these well-established rules. Now, in the GATS context, China has made commitments when it comes to service-based sectors for online services and value-added telecommunications, among others, and it's also liberalized numerous sectors where goods and services can be traded online.

In 2011, USTR communicated with their Chinese counterparts about this, inquiring as to the regulatory basis and other GATS related compliance to these sorts of unpublished guidelines. The, I think, 2013 National Trade Estimate report indicated that in 2012, USTR had further communications with China about regulating in a transparent fashion. That's all the information that I have at present, but from the evidence that we see today, that hasn't led to any change in regulatory policy.

Now, it is the case that exceptions exist to GATS that states can violate their trade commitments. In certain cases, such as with respect to public morals and public order, the international trade regime does contemplate that there may be cases where this is necessary, but those cases are narrow.

They need to be necessary to achieve the stated objective, and they can only be taken when there's no less restrictive alternative for achieving the same goal, and they need to be applied without prejudice, and, of course, the procedural oversights and opportunities for review that I mentioned also apply.

The sort of unannounced arbitrary and often random or seemingly random blocking of online services doesn't comport with these obligations. Recent WTO rulings reinforce this. The online gambling case and the audio-visuals case both demonstrate that, one, these obligations apply in the online environment, and culturally sensitive issues are not a get-out-of-jail-free card when it comes to WTO obligations.

So, in conclusion, let me just say the question of whether or not international trade rules are violated by Internet censorship is not really a legal question any longer. Trade law scholars agreed years ago that it is a violation of international trade law obligations.

From the U.S. perspective, the question is really whether or not the U.S. can politically afford to make a trade dispute over online censorship, and to that I would respond: given the growing importance of the Internet to the U.S. economy, the question is no longer whether we can afford to, but for how long can we afford not to make this a trade issue?

Thanks for your time. I appreciate the opportunity, and I look forward to your questions.

PREPARED STATEMENT OF MATTHEW SCHRUERS, VICE PRESIDENT FOR LAW & POLICY, COMPUTER & COMMUNICATIONS INDUSTRY ASSOCIATION

Commercial Espionage and Barriers to Digital Trade in China

June 15, 2015

Testimony before the U.S.-China Economic and Security Review Commission

Matt Schruers
Vice President, Law & Policy
Computer & Communications Industry Association

On behalf of the Computer & Communications Industry Association (CCIA), I thank you for the opportunity to discuss digital barriers to trade in China today. CCIA is a trade association of Internet and technology firms that has promoted openness, competition, and free trade for over 40 years. We appreciate the Commission's attention to this matter, which is crucial to U.S. economic and political interests.

Barriers to digital trade in China have been and continue to be a significant challenge for U.S. business. Worldwide, the U.S. business community is on the front lines in the battle against censoring, filtering, and blocking of Internet content, and for years it confronted these problems with only limited support from the U.S. Government. This is very much the case with respect to China as well. Because the business community has a limited capacity to respond to other nations' interference with the cross-border flow of services, products, and information, it is up to governments to lead in the defense of Internet freedom and free trade principles.

I. Benefits of digital trade to the U.S. economy

Traditionally, online freedoms have rightly been viewed through the lens of human rights, and CCIA supports the efforts by many stakeholders, including intergovernmental and non-governmental organizations, to encourage nations to meet human rights norms in this area. As explained here, however, restrictions on the free flow of information online have serious *economic* consequences in addition to the injury they do to human rights.

The Internet's contribution to the U.S. economy is vast. It now exceeds the contribution of agriculture, arts, entertainment and recreation, and construction, among other traditional industries. It has also surpassed the contribution of the U.S. Federal Government, and by 2016 is estimated to reach $4.2 trillion across all G-20 economies.[1] The Internet is also one of the great success stories for U.S. exports. U.S. exports of digitally enabled services grew from $282.1 billion in 2007 to $356.1 billion in 2011, with exports exceeding imports every year during that period.[2]

Digitally facilitated trade is not merely an issue for large technology firms; the inhibition of cross-border flow of information services is important to large and small companies alike. The World Economic Forum concluded that the Internet "can be a powerful tool to unlock SME ('small and medium-sized enterprises') export potential, and that removing barriers to Internet- enabled international trade could increase cross-border opportunities for small businesses by 60% to 80%."[3] Research shows that technology-enabled SMEs demonstrate higher survival rates,[4] and SMEs who heavily utilized the Internet export twice as much as

---

[1] David Dean *et al.*, Boston Consulting Group, *The Connected World: The $4.2 Trillion Opportunity - The Internet Economy in the G-20* (2012), at 3, 49, https://www.bcg.com/documents/file100409.pdf.
[2] U.S. International Trade Commission, *Digital Trade in the U.S. and Global Economies, Part 1* (2013), http://www.usitc.gov/press_room/news_release/2013/er0815ll1.htm.
[3] World Economic Forum, *Enabling Trade, Valuing Growth Opportunities* (2013), at 19-20, http://www.weforum.org/reports/enabling-trade-valuing-growth-opportunities.
[4] eBay, *Commerce 3.0 for Development: The promise of the Global Empowerment Network* (2013), http://www.ebaymainstreet.com/news-events/commerce-30-development-promise-global-empowerment-network.

those that did not, and further, Internet usage increased SME productivity by 10%.[5]

The Internet has fundamentally transformed the entire business value chain in virtually all sectors and for all types of companies.[6] According to the OECD, the Internet is a "general purpose technology enabler," which is defined as a once-in-a-generation technology that reorganizes world economic activity and spurs productivity. In fact, the OECD expects the positive effects of the Internet to surpass those of prior general purpose technology enablers, such as the printing press, the steam engine and the electrical grid.[7]

In light of the extraordinary potential that Internet-enabled trade has for the U.S. economy, maintaining a level playing field should be a U.S. priority. Unfortunately, it is often the case that businesses in China and other nations that engage in filtering, blocking, and censorship of U.S. digital trade have full access to the U.S. market. In discussing the protectionist impulses and unequal treatment of U.S. and Chinese firms in the Chinese market several years ago, a *Foreign Policy* article observed:

> Even a seemingly harmless site, like photo-sharing website Flickr, has been blocked in China, while its identical clone Bababian has grown steadily with foreign technology and no foreign competition. Likewise, blog-hosting sites Blogger and WordPress have long been blocked in China. Instead, Chinese netizens use Tianya, the 13th-most popular site in China. Far from being a sanitized land of boring blogs about daily activities, Tianya also hosts China's largest Internet forum, a vitriolic, sensationalized, and hate- filled arena that makes Western gossip sites seem like the Economist. In the face of an obvious and systematic form of protectionism in perhaps the most important industry for the future, the cheering from many leading American figures for Google's "brave" decision [to exit the Chinese market] seems strange. If China were attempting to block the import of American tires, instead of American Internet media, would Americans applaud Goodyear and Congress for not putting up a fight against blatant WTO violations?[8]

Unfortunately, little has changed in the intervening period. It should be a serious concern for U.S. policymakers that American technology companies do not enjoy the same unfettered access, especially as the Chinese market continues to expand. It is estimated that as of 2014, China has 632 million Internet users — the world's largest Internet market.[9] Ambassador Froman remarked recently that the Asian-Pacific middle class is growing drastically. As of 2009, there were 525 million middle class consumers in Asia. That number is estimated to

---

[5] McKinsey Global Institute, *Internet Matters: The Net's sweeping impact on growth, jobs and prosperity*, May 2011.

[6] McKinsey Global Institute, *The Great Transformer: The Impact of the Internet on Economic Growth and Prosperity*, Oct. 2011, http://www.mckinsey.com/insights/high_tech_telecoms_internet/the_great_transformer.

[7] OECD, *Broadband and the Economy, Ministerial Background Report*, May 2007, http://www.oecd.org/sti/40781696.pdf.

[8] Jordan Calinoff, *Beijing's Foreign Internet Purge*, Foreign Policy, Jan. 15, 2010, http://foreignpolicy.com/2010/01/15/beijings-foreign-internet-purge/.

[9] McKinsey Global Institute, *China's Digital Transformation: The Internet's Impact on Productivity and Growth*, July 2014.

grow to 3.2 billion by 2030.[10] It is not only the growing consumer base that makes the Chinese market a relevant area for growth, but also the dramatic rise of Internet connections. E-commerce for consumer electronics posted a compound annual growth rate of 103 percent from 2009 to 2012. The McKinsey Global Institute developed an "iGDP" indicator to measure the size of a country's Internet economy and noted that in 2010, China's Internet economy stood at 3.3 percent of its GDP, and by 2013, its iGDP had reached 4.4 percent, moving China into the ranks of the global leaders.[11] In reference to this metric, China's Internet economy is already larger than those of the United States, France, and Germany as a share of GDP.[12]

Chinese companies are capitalizing on their thriving market and becoming increasingly competitive on a global scale. As of May 2015, four Chinese companies were included in the top 15 global public Internet companies (ranked by market capitalization), whereas none were in 1995.[13] While Chinese companies enjoy growth bolstered by unrestricted market access at home and abroad, U.S. companies face a more saturated home market, with lower growth rates. In the late 90s and early 2000s U.S. companies faced a scalable, expanding market that was early in the adoption cycle, making it easier to overlook foreign competitors. Today those same competitors cannot be ignored. Not only is the U.S. facing a mere 2 percent expansion rate of Internet growth, but 79% of the users of the top 10 Internet platforms come from outside the United States.[14] This number is expected to grow in the future. Furthermore, major Chinese Internet companies have announced global expansion plans, many targeting the U.S. market.[15]

As an association that has committed several decades to the defense of competition, open markets and free trade, CCIA welcomes the emergence and growth of Chinese Internet companies. The internationalization of Internet innovation is a boon to global consumers and drives further innovation. However, with global aspirations comes a responsibility to abide by international norms, especially for WTO members who enjoy the benefits of open markets and free trade.

II. How filtering, blocking, and censorship affects U.S. commerce

---

[10] Remarks by Ambassador Michael Froman at the U.S. Conference of Mayors (Jan. 2015), https://ustr.gov/about- us/policy-offices/press-office/speechestranscripts/2015/january/remarks-ambassador-froman-us.

[11] *Id.* at 2. "The iGDP indicator uses the expenditure method of calculating GDP. It totals all activities linked to the creation and use of Internet networks and services: consumption by individuals (including hardware, software, Internet access, and e-commerce), public expenditure (including infrastructure), business investment in Internet technologies, and the country's trade balance in Internet-related goods and services."

[12] *Id.* at 3.

[13] Mary Meeker, *2015 Internet Trends* (May 2015), http://www.kpcb.com/internet-trends.

[14] Mary Meeker, *2014 Internet Trends* (May 2014), http://kpcbweb2.s3.amazonaws.com/files/85/Internet_Trends_2014_vFINAL_-_05_28_14-_PDF.pdf?1401286773#page=130.

[15] Jessica Guynn, *Is Alibaba coming to America?*, USA Today, Sept. 17, 2014, http://www.usatoday.com/story/tech/2014/09/16/alibaba-ipo-expansion-united-states-europe/15736493/;   Josh Ong, *China's Tencent lays groundwork to expand its popular WeChat messaging app to US*, Next Web, Feb. 26, 2013, http://thenextweb.com/asia/2013/02/26/chinas-tencent-creates-wechat-task-force-to-research-us-expansion/.

While methods for filtering, blocking, or censoring U.S. services vary, they typically consist of (a) the imposition of legal or regulatory obligations upon intermediaries, which may include blocking access to an entire Internet service or specific keywords, web pages, and domains, requiring Internet search engines to disappear search results; (b) similar blocking and/or filtering as may be required of an online service, but executed pursuant to unpublished and unappealable orders at the network level through state control or influence over the communications infrastructure; or (c) technology mandates that either hobble user privacy and security, or that force product manufacturers to include intrusive monitoring technology or back-doors.

China has implemented these various techniques not only against foreign websites, known aptly as the "Great Firewall of China," but to a lesser extent domestically as well. Some have explained the elaborate Chinese censorship system as being geared towards maximizing the economic benefits of the Internet while maintaining strict social control. Whatever the domestic aim of these mechanisms may be, they function, intentionally or not, as unlawful barriers to international trade.

For many years, U.S. sites, platforms and services have been intermittently or persistently blocked at the network level, often over relatively trivial content or for "dubious" reasons.[16] Chinese authorities have been known to redirect traffic from U.S.-based search engines to Baidu, their China-based competitor,[17] and Baidu's share of the Chinese search market has increased.

More recently, this discriminatory treatment escalated even further, with analytics traffic in China being redirected *from* Baidu at the network level toward U.S. sites as a form of malicious distributed denial of service ("DDoS"). Victims included GitHub, a platform popular among programmers, and the censorship-tracking site GreatFire, both of which provided tools that allow Chinese citizens to circumvent network-level censorship.[18] This event followed soon after Chinese authorities announced a new initiative to "guide Internet-based companies to increase their presence in the international market."[19]

As the U.S. International Trade Commission's 2013 report noted, China was found to be a pervasive censor of Internet content in reports by at least three separate NGOs: the Open Network Initiative, Freedom House, and Reporters Without Borders. (The ITC report also identified 12 other countries that at least 2 of those 3 organizations characterized as Internet

---

[16] *See, e.g.*, Claudine Beaumont, *Foursquare Blocked in China*, The Telegraph, June 4, 2010, http://www.telegraph.co.uk/technology/socialmedia/7802992/Foursquare-blocked-in-China.html.   *See* Calinoff, *supra* note 8.

[17] John Biggs, *Cyberwar: China Declares War On Western Search Sites*, TechCrunch, Oct. 18, 2007, http://techcrunch.com/2007/10/18/cyberwar-china-declares-war-on-western-search-sites/.

[18] Russell Brandom, *China's 'Great Cannon' Can Intercept and Redirect Web Traffic*, The Verge, Apr. 10, 2015, http://www.theverge.com/2015/4/10/8381827/china-great-cannon-firewall-web-censorship; Nicol Perlroth, *China Is Said to Use Powerful New Weapon to Censor Internet*, Apr. 10, 2015, http://www.nytimes.com/2015/04/11/technology/china-is-said-to-use-powerful-new-weapon-to-censor-internet.html.

[19] *Id.*

censors.)[20] Reflecting the impact of this ongoing discriminatory treatment, U.S. services have "been systematically forced out of the [Chinese] market" over time.[21]

While many U.S. Internet companies are effectively blocked from the Chinese market, their Chinese Internet competitors not only have access to U.S. markets, but rely on them to engage leading providers of financial, legal, and technical services, as well as U.S. hardware. Chinese

Internet firms enjoy the benefits of a walled-off home market to grow and achieve scale, after which they frequently turn to U.S. capital markets and employ U.S.-based underwriters to fund their continued growth and expansion in both their domestic markets and into international markets. In September 2014, the Hangzhou-based e-commerce and internet platform Alibaba completed the largest IPO in NYSE history, raising more than $21 billion.[22] Four major U.S. headquartered banks (Goldman Sachs, JPMorgan Chase, Morgan Stanley and Citigroup) participated in the deal as lead underwriters.[23] Alibaba — now the third most valuable Internet company in the world, ahead of Amazon and Yahoo![24] — has also announced plans to expand into U.S. and European markets.[25]

Alibaba was not unique. In 2005, Baidu, China's largest search engine (who was able to scale in its home market after Google was effectively blocked from the Chinese market) raised $109 million dollars and utilized Goldman Sachs and Piper Jaffray as underwriters.[26] Weibo and Renren, often described as clones of popular American social media sites, are other examples of major Chinese Internet companies that raised money on U.S. stock exchanges and used American financial firms to underwrite the process.[27]

It bears noting that while these strategies are practiced within China, they are also practiced by other nations as well, with the result being that U.S. services are allowed uneven and unequal access to numerous growing markets abroad. Because for many years the United States has largely acquiesced to digital trade barriers in China, other governments have been emboldened to follow this lead. As a result, Internet services — one of the fastest growing areas of U.S.

---

[20] United States International Trade Commission Investigation, *Digital Trade in the U.S. and Global Economies, Part 1,* Investigation No. 332-531. USITC Publication 4415. July 2013. http://www.usitc.gov/publications/332/pub4415.pdf#page=175.

[21] *See* Calinoff, *supra* note 8; Ellen Nakashima & Cecilia Kang, *In Response to New Rules, GoDaddy To Stop Registering Domain Names in China,* Washington Post, March 25, 2010, http://www.washingtonpost.com/wp-dyn/content/article/2010/03/24/AR2010032401543.html; Zach Miners, *Yahoo Exits China, Closing R&D Center,* InfoWorld, Mar. 19, 2015, http://www.infoworld.com/article/2899056/technology-business/yahoo-exits-china- closing-randd-center.html.

[22] Michael J. de la Merced, *Alibaba Raises $21.8 Billion in Initial Public Offering,* DealBook, Sept. 18, 2014, http://dealbook.nytimes.com/2014/09/18/alibaba-raises-21-8-billion-in-initial-public-offering/.

[23] Michael J. de la Merced, *The Six Banks Leading Alibaba's Giant I.P.O.,* DealBook, May 6, 2014, http://dealbook.nytimes.com/2014/05/06/the-six-banks-who-are-leading-alibabas-giant-i-p-o/.

[24] Mary Meeker, *2015 Internet Trends, supra* note 13.

[25] Guynn, *Is Alibaba coming to America?, supra* note 15.

[26] Steve Gelsi, *Baidu.com more than triples,* MarketWatch, Aug 5, 2005, http://www.marketwatch.com/story/baidu- ipo-jumps-354-into-the-record-books.

[27] Claire Baldwin & Jennifer Saba, *Renren's big day, maybe a prelude to Facebook IPO,* Reuters, May 4, 2011, http://www.reuters.com/article/2011/05/05/us-renren-ipo-idUSTRE7433HI20110505; Renaissance Capital, *Weibo prices downsized IPO at $17, at the low end of the range,* Nasdaq, Apr. 16, 2014, http://www.nasdaq.com/article/weibo-prices-downsized-ipo-at-17-at-the-low-end-of-the-range-cm345076.

exports
— face one of the most hostile market landscapes abroad.

III. Mechanisms governing barriers to international trade

Domestic and international law has long sought to ensure that the cross-border trade in goods and services is liberalized and free from unnecessary or protectionist restrictions. Promoting free markets across the world remains a key U.S. economic objective, and as the United States transitions into a global information economy where U.S. businesses are positioned to be leading vendors of products and services, this objective becomes even more important.

A variety of international instruments exist to guarantee the global free trade in goods and services. The generally open nature of international trade today is a legacy of efforts that began more than 60 years ago, with the General Agreement on Tariffs and Trade (GATT), which liberalized trade in goods in the mid-20th century. More recently, this framework was subsumed into the World Trade Organization (WTO) and was followed by services liberalization under the General Agreement on Trade in Services (GATS). GATT was aimed at removing market access impediments and non-tariff barriers, establishing baseline principles for free trade such as non- discrimination and national treatment. As a result, foreign goods (and following GATS, services) must receive treatment at least equal to that given to domestic equivalents in WTO- compliant countries.

GATS similarly requires participating nations to abide by principles of non-discrimination and national treatment with respect to services, and also enforces rules such as fair market access, and transparency and impartiality in the administration of rules. GATS also includes a Telecommunications Annex which makes clear that non-discrimination obligations include access to and use of public telecommunications networks. Violations of these obligations may be addressed through the WTO's dispute resolution mechanisms.

Similar obligations, applying market access principles to the cross-border provision of online services and e-commerce, have been discussed in the context of ongoing plurilateral trade agreement talks, including the Trans-Pacific Partnership, the Transatlantic Trade and Investment Partnership, and the Trade in Services Agreement. Domestically, U.S. law also provides mechanisms aimed at securing open markets for the export of U.S. goods and services, administered by the U.S. Trade Representative. In this vein, USTR announced a digital trade policy in May 2015 anchored in 12 principles to promote a free and open Internet. Several of the principles, such as securing basic non-discrimination commitments and enabling cross-border data flows, speak directly to the concerns at issue here.[28]

---

[28] U.S. Trade Representative, *The Digital Dozen* (May 2015), https://ustr.gov/sites/default/files/USTR-The_Digital_Dozen.pdf.

IV. How online filtering, blocking, and censorship violate international trade obligations

As noted above, restrictions on Internet content and services may be prohibited by both GATT and GATS. The remainder of this section identified relevant aspects of those two instruments.

   A. GATT

While the function of GATT was to liberalize trade in physical goods, law and legal scholarship still admits for the possibility of applying those commitments in the digital context. It is certainly the case that online services which implicate neither downloaded nor stored goods, such as search and social media, must be considered "services," analyzed with reference to GATS, not GATT. Nevertheless, disagreements remain regarding products that are downloaded, and kept in digital form, "like newspapers, songs, software, audio and electronic books. While the WTO has yet to rule on the issues, or its members to agree, the better position is that the digital versions of goods remain goods subject to GATT."[29] In any event, physical goods may be purchased through digital means, and thereby implicating the objectives embodied in GATT.

GATT requires a contracting party to afford goods supplied from abroad similar status to like products originating from domestic suppliers.[30] Yet in many cases platforms and services through which digital products can be obtained are subjected to specific censorship that provides a competitive advantage to similar products originating in China. Certain U.S. social media services, for example, have been completely blocked in China, while their Chinese equivalents Weibo and Renren are allowed to operate with selective filtering.

GATT similarly requires "[l]aws, regulations, judicial decisions and administrative rulings of general application" to be published promptly, and to be administered in a "uniform, impartial and reasonable manner."[31] The filtering, blocking, and censorship that U.S. services encounter, however, generally remains unpublished and unevenly applied. Moreover, little legal recourse exists to dispute the administration of such measures. As a 2011 information request from the U.S. Trade Representative to Chinese counterparts pursuant to GATS Article III suggested, U.S. businesses subject to filtering, blocking, or censoring in China often are subjected to unpublished (or arbitrary) guidelines and criteria which are neither public nor published, nor developed in a transparent fashion.[32]

   B. GATS

Even if GATT is construed to not reach digital trade, numerous provisions of GATS prohibit the filtering, blocking, and censorship that is applied to Internet services. GATS imposes

---

[29] Tim Wu, *The World Trade Law of Censorship and Filtering* (May 2006), *at* http://ssrn.com/abstract=882459, at 7.
[30] GATT Art. III:4 (1947 text).
[31] GATT Arts. X:1, X:3(a)-(b).
[32] Office of the United States Trade Representative, *United States Seeks Detailed Information on China's Internet Restrictions* (Oct. 2011), https://ustr.gov/about-us/policy-offices/press-office/press-releases/2011/october/united-   states-seeks-detailed-information-china's-i.

considerable obligations on WTO Members, mandating transparency, impartiality, and non-discrimination in trade-related government actions, and requires that affected parties be afforded opportunities for judicial or independent review of trade-related administrative decisions. While exceptions to these obligations exist, such as for "public morals/order"[33] GATS derogations are only permissible when necessary to achieve the stated objective, where no reasonable, less restrictive alternative exists, and when applied without prejudice.[34] Where nations implement filtering, blocking, and censoring of online services, these standards are rarely met.

It is necessary to note that whereas GATT imposes blanket commitments, GATS governs sectors and "modes" where a contracting party has made specific commitments. The Chinese Government has made specific commitments pertaining to various web-based service sectors, however, as well as value-added telecommunications.[35]

As with GATT, GATS requires reasonable publication and impartial administration of trade-related regulatory measures. When U.S. services encounter arbitrary restrictions, often at odds with what domestic competitors are subjected to, it likely constitutes a GATS violation.[36] The market access commitments contained in GATS Article XVI also apply in this context.

Following the WTO *Online Gambling* dispute between the United States and Antigua, it is clear that once a contracting party has agreed to liberalize a given mode of service supply, it may not continue to maintain bans in that sector absent some rationale for doing so that comports with the GATS exceptions. The *Online Gambling* case establishes that such service bans should be considered "zero quotas," and quantitative restrictions of this nature are prohibited in liberalized sectors by GATS Article XVI.[37] This outcome leads to the further conclusion that "that many WTO member states are legally obliged to permit an unrestricted supply of cross-border Internet services," and that even states claiming public morals exemptions to justify censorship cannot persistently block general purpose online services and remain compliant with their GATS obligations.[38]

As the recent dispute between the United States and China regarding regulation of imports and distribution of publications and audiovisual products shows, a government's desire to control online content does not enable it to ignore WTO rules.[39] In the *Audiovisuals* case, China sought to justify restrictions on foreign investment for the import and distribution of books,

---

[33] Exceptions for "public morals"/"public order" may be found in GATT Art. XX(a) and GATS Art. XIV(a).
[34] GATS Art. XIV. *See* Tim Wu, *The World Trade Law of Censorship and Filtering* (May 2006), http://ssrn.com/abstract=882459, at 13.
[35] Frederik Erixon, Brian Hindley, & Hosuk Lee-Makiyama, *Protectionism Online: Internet Censorship and International Trade Law* (2009), http://www.ecipe.org/publications/protectionism-online-internet-censorship-and- international-trade-law/.
[36] GATS Art. XVII:1.
[37] Tim Wu, *The World Trade Law of Censorship and Filtering* (May 2006), http://ssrn.com/abstract=882459. *See* Frederik Erixon, Brian Hindley, & Hosuk Lee-Makiyama, *Protectionism Online: Internet Censorship and International Trade Law* (2009), http://www.ecipe.org/publications/protectionism-online-internet-censorship-and- international-trade-law/, at 9.
[38] Erixon *et al.*, *supra.*
[39] Appellate Body Report, *China – Publications and Audiovisual Products* (Dec. 21, 2009); Panel Report, *China – Publications and Audiovisual Products* (Aug. 12, 2009).

movies, and other "culturally sensitive" materials because it wanted to protect public morals and control content. There remains little question today that the "public morals" exception allows only for narrowly tailored restrictions in certain special cases, and does not constitute a free pass.[40]

V.   Conclusion

To criticize foreign filtering, blocking, and censorship is not to say that U.S. policy should resist open competition from Chinese Internet firms in the free market. On the contrary: one need only look at the amazing competition-driven progress in services like search, social media, and e- commerce to appreciate how robust competition drives firms to innovate, improving consumer welfare and benefiting society. This competition cannot occur when governments intercede in the marketplace to suppress foreign competitors and benefit local incumbents. Whether such intervention is in fact motivated by "public morals" concerns or is merely protectionism clothed as such, is ultimately irrelevant if it violates international commitments. Accordingly, international remedies can and should be explored as a means for ensuring the free and open exchange of information online.

---

[40] *Id.*

OPENING STATEMENT OF SAMM SACKS, CHINA ANALYST, EURASIA GROUP

MS. SACKS: Thank you for the opportunity to testify today.

I think that we are at a critical moment in which the landscape for foreign technology companies, and specifically for ICT companies, is fundamentally changing with significant impact for the business landscape. This is a good time.

What I would like to do in my testimony is focus on three points, why I see a new operating environment for these firms and also to clear up two misconceptions. The first is that we could potentially see Beijing walk back on some of the policies that are out there today, and the second is that I do not see the environment being prohibited for foreign technology firms in China, and I'd like to talk about where I see some of those opportunities. And last, I'll close with some recommendations.

On the first point, I think we're in an environment in which the Chinese government is linking localization with national security and cybersecurity. Foreign firms now more than any other time face greater risks of invasive security audits, that they will be compelled to build local data centers, provide the Chinese government with encryption access, and to turn over source code.

This is part of the high level effort by the Xi Jinping government with the goal of gaining more oversight and control of foreign technology. Now, as several people today have mentioned, this is not the first time in which we have seen this effort. Indigenous innovation as a concept has been around for years, but I think that the landscape is different now than it is in the past.

The Chinese government is pressing forward with both formal and with informal policy mechanisms in order to achieve these goals.

I'll briefly outline some of the formal policy tools and would be happy to go into more depth in the Q&A on any of these items.

There are a number of laws, regulations and frameworks that have either been released in draft form or are rumored to exist. The first is a counterterrorism law, which we believe will be passed this year, requiring encryption access and data localization. There are restrictions on foreign technology in the banking IT sector requiring suppliers to meet standards for secure and controllable technologies. A national security law has been released in draft form. Two worrying provisions of that include cyber sovereignty as well as national security review bodies.

There is a Five-Year Plan for the ICT sector and numerous other cybersecurity laws that are all moving forward.

We are also seeing on the informal side a push to pressure purchasers in China to buy from local providers as well as foreign companies being compelled to submit to IP and technology inspections.

How is this different from the past? First, we see the Xi Jinping administration centralizing political capacity, providing added weight to actually implement these in a way that we have not seen in the past. The Leading Small Group for Network Security and Informatization is emerging as one of the most powerful players in the Chinese bureaucracy today. It has been elevated to a Party level, which is different from its predecessor under the Hu Jintao administration. Half of the members of this group are ranked at the most senior levels across the Party, military and government.

That's not to say that Chinese policymaking system is monolithic. There are very strong voices opposing some of these policies, but they have been sidelined and the hardliners have been somewhat empowered in this environment.

There's reason to believe that there's not full consensus behind these policies as a number of these policies will hurt Chinese industry and banks with added security compliance requirements. The idea that a provider would be chosen based on localization as opposed to security will expose security risks in critical Chinese infrastructure and financial institutions and industry as well as stifle innovation for Chinese companies.

But we think that the Chinese government is using the top-down approach in which its own industrial stakeholders have had limited input and consultation in this policy process.

I do not think that these policies are going away. There has been speculation that the counterterrorism law was perhaps going to be suspended earlier this spring. That's not the case. We're now hearing reports, credible reports that policymakers are under pressure to accelerate passage of the counterterrorism law this year. The banking IT regulations have been temporarily suspended, but they will be revisited.

Another reason why we see a more concerted effort to push forward this policy agenda is that the Xi Jinping administration is pushing harder on promoting domestic industry than its predecessors. We see an unprecedented effort in terms of scale, levels of government backing, the vision of these plans in order to groom domestic industry.

The Made in China 2025 Plan, the Internet Plus Plan, a number of integrated circuit support plans over the past year confirm this, and I'd be happy to speak about any of those in more detail.

But the other misconception out there is that Beijing has no interest in fully prohibiting foreign technology companies from China, and in fact I spend a lot of my day at Eurasia Group working closely with companies on how to navigate this market. I still believe that Beijing recognizes foreign expertise and technology is critical to their national goals for upgrading domestic industry, for creating jobs as the economy slows, and, in fact, even if you look at the Made in China 2025 Plan, there's an explicit call for more joint research and development.

So the trick for U.S. companies is how to navigate this environment in which the formal barriers to market entry are lowering, even in some sensitive sectors, at the same time you still have increased market costs of being in those sectors.

I think that there are three main goals that the U.S. government should focus on:

The first is given that these policies are likely to move forward, the goal should be to have the language of these policies be as broad and discretionary as possible with the goal of leaving U.S. companies room for maneuverability. There should be a spectrum in how these policies are implemented, and that's where it will be important to find space.

The second is conveying to the Chinese government the ways in which these policies are undermining their own goals for technology innovation among Chinese companies for added compliance costs and, most importantly, the security risks to their own critical infrastructure that are exposed through localization.

And third, I think that it's important that we develop a common set of practices and best approaches with international partners as we approach this market landscape.

I look forward to your questions. Thank you.

PREPARED STATEMENT SAMM SACKS, CHINA ANALYST, EURASIA GROUP

Testimony before the U.S.-China Economic and Security Review Commission:
Regulatory Barriers to Digital Trade in China, and Costs to US Firms

Key take-aways

- The Chinese government will press forward with stricter scrutiny of US technology suppliers given a determination on the part of the Xi Jinping government to deliver on long-held national security and domestic industrial innovation goals.
- The counterterrorism law and banking sector information technology (IT) regulations both remain in play despite reports to the contrary.
- US technology companies face greater risks now that they will be required to undergo invasive security audits, turn over source code, build local data centers, and provide the Chinese government with encryption access under a number of laws and policy directives.
- The Central Leading Small Group for Network Security and Informatization set up in February 2014 and chaired by President Xi is emerging as one of the most powerful elements within the bureaucracy and will consolidate the leadership's power to push forward national policies.
- Although hardliners have been empowered to shape China's foreign technology policies, China's political system is not monolithic. Some groups think localization will expose Chinese government and financial institution networks to security risks, while added compliance costs will impede innovation for emerging Chinese companies.
- A lack of full consensus, added security and compliance costs to Chinese industry and banks, and technological barriers for implementation mean that US firms will not lose market share at the pace and to the degree that some fear.
- Over the past year the Xi administration has shown a serious commitment to indigenous technological development that is unprecedented in scale, high-levels of government backing, approach, and vision—suggesting that China could show more progress on this front than in the past.
- But US firms will have to weigh the benefits of market access with added local data storage requirements, IP risks surrounding new licensing approvals, security reviews especially in online data transmission, and other forms of "soft discrimination."
- US policymakers and regulators should convey to the Chinese government the ways in which a hardline approach undermines objectives of President Xi's economic policy agenda – and how such policies can hinder Chinese companies as well as US companies.
- The US government should seek dialogue with Beijing with the goal of US companies having space for maneuverability in the final policy language, rather than provoking Beijing to dig in deeper and leave US companies with limited options for operating in China's market.
- The US government should also cooperate with other countries on developing a common set of best practices and guidance for operating in the China market.

Beijing appears unlikely to back down on IT policies requirements despite US pressure

The Chinese government will press forward with stricter scrutiny of foreign technology suppliers given a determination on the part of the Xi Jinping government to deliver on long-held national security and domestic industry goals. While there could be some room for compromise about timing, the extent of implementation for new requirements, and perhaps some of the ways in which these initiatives are implemented, Beijing is not likely to back down on its push to have more rigorous oversight and control over technology and information security, an area that has important implications for foreign intellectual property (IP). These development are leading to a fundamental shift in the business climate for US companies in a range of technology sectors, particularly for information technology (IT) but also in finance, next generation manufacturing, and energy efficiency.

Recent initiatives reinforce three distinct, high-level objectives by the Xi leadership. First, the government has a genuine concern about national security vulnerabilities as exposed in the Edward Snowden revelations in 2013. Second, President Xi has signaled a new commitment to driving technology innovation among Chinese industry as the government seeks to shift toward high value-add growth and promote the competitiveness of Chinese companies. Third, the government is expanding efforts to strengthen data security in the face of a rapid explosion in e-commerce, big data, and information transmission over the internet more broadly as it consolidates power. The Chinese government also is critical of the US for having double standards, maintaining that requiring encryption access is consistent with global standards.

There has been speculation in recent months about how far Beijing will go with localization efforts and plans to increase control over foreign technology. In March the US media reported that the counterterrorism law under review had been suspended following concerns raised by President Obama to President Xi; in April Beijing announced it would temporarily halt rules that increased restrictions on banks and their IT suppliers. But both policies remain in play despite reports to the contrary. In fact, there are now credible rumors that government officials are facing pressure to accelerate passage of the counterterrorism law this year, and the banking sector regulations are likely to be revisited as well.

Formal and informal tools to gain more oversight and control over foreign technology

Even if some parts of the regulations are diluted, Beijing is pressing forward with a spate of formal and informal tools that taken together will allow the government to assert more control and increase security and regulatory scrutiny of US technology companies in the next one to two years. US technology companies face greater risks that they will be required to undergo invasive audits, turn over source code, and provide the Chinese government with encryption keys for surveillance. Key legislation and policy directives that have emerged, are in draft, or are widely rumored include:

- A purge of foreign firms from a government-sanctioned procurement lists
- Restrictions on foreign equipment in the banking sector requiring suppliers to meet "secure and controllable" standards

- A draft counterterrorism law compelling telecom and internet companies to provide encryption keys to enable government surveillance and store data on local Chinese servers
- A new national security law that will expand Beijing's regulatory powers under a broad and far-reaching definition of national security and calls for sovereignty in cyberspace
- The creation of a cyberspace review body to evaluate security for all internet and IT products
- A new cybersecurity law or framework
- A 13th Five Year Plan for Software and Big data focused on boosting data security for SOEs, financial institutions, and government agencies

Among the laws currently under consideration, the counterterrorism law is perhaps the focus of the most high-level political attention right now that will increase the likelihood of its passage in the coming year. It is possible that Beijing could walk back the encryption access and localization requirements in the final version of the law, and use broad language that leaves space for discretion when it comes to implementation. However this alone would not mitigate risks to foreign firms given the overall policy environment and inclinations of the top leadership.

A second draft of the national security law came out in early May and is likely to be passed next year. Once enacted, this law will serve as the legal framework to bolster security across all sectors of the economy, including but not limited to internet and information technologies. While the final content of the law is not yet known, draft language reveal two worrisome developments. First, the provision of the law calling for cyberspace sovereignty suggests that the Chinese government is pursuing a policy strategy that could eventually over the long-term lead to fragmentation of the US-led global internet. Beijing is seeking to have a greater ability to control internet content as a tool to maintain stability. Second, this law is likely to serve as the legal basis for national security reviews of inbound investment—also proposed in the draft foreign investment law still under review—and could also lead to the creation of new bodies nationwide, akin to the Committee on Foreign Investment in the United States (CFIUS). Currently these security review bodies only exist within China's four free trade zones (FTZs) in Fujian, Tianjin, Guangdong, and Shanghai under a new pilot announced just in April. But initial content readings of the draft law suggest that these new bodies will take a more expansive approach to national security than CFIUS, providing justification for restricting foreign investment across sectors on the basis of strategic, economic, social, moral, ideological, and technical readings of national security.

The pace of cybersecurity policymaking is also accelerating in ways that suggest Beijing will look to assert greater sovereignty in cyberspace. Although drafting of the cybersecurity law or guiding framework is not as far along as that of the counterterrorism and national security law, Premier Li Keqiang indicated at the National People's Congress in March that completing a first draft would be a priority for 2015. In May the Ministry of Industry and Information Technology announced it will draft a five year plan for the ICT sector focused on improving network security, innovation, and global competitiveness. That same month the Shanghai Academy of Social Sciences (SASS) released its annual report on cybersecurity expressing concern that the US has too much influence over global cyber space and seeks to contain China's technology development. The SASS report—a full book length volume—provides a detailed compendium with research on topics including: security risks with next generation IT systems, developing policies and laws in cyberspace, online cultural security, development of the information security industry in an era of big data, and global internet governance.

Outside of formal policy channels, the government will take a more assertive approach to requiring companies to submit technology and IP for inspection. Purchasers may also face more pressure to buy domestic. State and quasi-state sponsored hacking methods will also be used to help Beijing achieve these goals. Government officials are also pressuring banks, SOEs, private and quasi-private companies, and public institutions to purchase from local suppliers regardless of official policy.

The government will also treat banking IT as infrastructure slated for increased state support as the economy slows. There are a growing number of Chinese banks that will require significant investment in IT systems (both hardware and software), providing an attractive venue for the government to achieve these goals. These banks will help to generate increased demand for equipment as the government focuses on redirecting state resources to build up the domestic IT sector. Chinese IT companies geared toward financial systems stand to gain from more policy support and incentives.

Hardliners on localization and cyber sovereignty empowered within bureaucracy

These latest developments reflect the growing influence of hardliners on China's industrial and foreign technology policies. Within the Chinese bureaucracy, proponents of greater data localization, import substitution, sovereignty in cyberspace, and encryption access are exerting increasing influence over the policy agenda. Hardline policies on these issues are not new to Chinese policy landscape and have in the past been walked back by Beijing—for example in 2007 the Ministry of Public Security introduced a "Multi-Level Protection Scheme" prohibiting foreign companies from supplying core products for government, banks, and other critical infrastructure companies; a 2010 "Compulsory Certification for Information Security Scheme" required foreign companies to submit security product IP to the government. But what is different now is that direction is coming from the highest levels in the Chinese system under the direction of President Xi himself.

The Central Leading Small Group for Network Security and Informatization set up in February 2014 and chaired by President Xi is emerging as one of the most powerful elements within the bureaucracy and will consolidate the leadership's power to push forward national policies. Contrary to popular perception, China's cyber policy environment had been fragmented among military, civilian, industrial, and other state actors at both regional and central levels, leading to gridlock and inconsistent implementation. This group is more powerful than its equivalent under the Hu administration. Xi himself is the chair while the earlier group was chaired by Premier Wen Jiabao. Elevating the group from the State Council level to the Party level will enable better coordination among the State Council, National People's Congress, and the People's Liberation Army.

Overall the make-up of the group suggests that development of the internet has become a focal point across the industrial, financial, and telecom space. Inclusion of departments such as the

National Development and Reform Commission, People's Bank of China, Ministry of Finance, and Ministry of Industry and Information Technology mean that there is support for boosting internet technologies across all areas of the bureaucracy. Of the 22 members of the group (President Xi and Premier Li Keqiang are the two top officials), roughly half have a status as the most senior rank among Party, military, and government officials.

But even as President Xi centralizes and consolidates power, it is important to keep in mind that China's political landscape is not monolithic and there are domestic players that are not necessarily supportive of the leadership's recent policy approach. A number of domestic companies have already voiced concerns to regulators, suggesting Beijing is using a top-down approach with limited consultation and input from industrial stakeholders. Chinese companies are concerned that local suppliers lag behind when it comes to securing infrastructure, and recognize that prioritizing localization rather than market competition around the most secure systems will expose Chinese networks to security risks. Huawei's rotating chief executive Eric Xu remarked in April that hampering competition will stifle innovation. Small start-ups also stand to lose from these policies since the new standards will demand more resources to be compliant.

IT policies also reflect an unprecedented effort to boost homegrown technology under President Xi

The Chinese government has talked about driving indigenous innovation and boosting homegrown technology industries for years, but has had limited success building competitive Chinese brands and shrinking the technology gap with foreign companies. Indigenous innovation policies under the administration of the former President Hu Jintao were largely ineffective, helping to maintain a status quo in which China's economy weighted heavily towards low-end manufacturing and energy and investment-intensive heavy industries, relying on foreign suppliers in value-add technology sectors.

But since coming to power in 2012, President Xi has made clear that China faces an imperative to shift the economy to a more sustainable and efficient mode of growth. A critical item on his reform agenda has been redirecting state resources toward high technology sectors seen as boosting consumer demand and upgrading Chinese industry to give value-add productivity a greater role in the economy. Over the past year the Xi administration has shown a serious commitment to technological development that is unprecedented in scale, high-levels of government backing, approach, and vision—suggesting that China could show more progress on this front than in the past.

Beijing is using the China Manufacturing 2025 Plan (unveiled on 19 May) together with the Internet Plus Strategy (introduced in March at the National People's Congress) as the main channels to promote local high value-add technology sectors as the economy slows. The aim is to drive economic growth by integrating internet and information technologies with traditional industries, strengthening global competiveness of Chinese companies, and reducing reliance on foreign technology. Under the Internet Plus strategy, Beijing will focus state funding and policy support on advancing smart technology, mobile internet, cloud computing, big data, the internet of things, and e-commerce. Traditional industries targeted for upgrades using internet technology include manufacturing, logistics, finance, and health. The Made in China plan targets ten key sectors for support such as next generation IT and intelligent manufacturing and robotics.

The scale of Beijing's ambitions are evident in specific industry support plans. There are also signs that recipients of this kind of state support will be selected based on potential for return on investment, consistent with reform goals to give market forces a greater role in the economy. For example, the State Council also announced in May that the government will invest over 1 trillion RMB over the next three years in building internet network infrastructure. In June 2014 the government announced it had set up a 120 billion RMB central government equity investment fund for the integrated circuits industry, which the Chinese government views as the critical bottleneck of China's domestic IT capabilities. Regions and municipalities are also setting up their own funds in addition. A national cloud-computing strategy released in January will encourage infrastructure upgrading for broadband and data centers and support domestic small- and medium enterprises (via preferential tax policies, financing, venture capital).

Separate Internet Plus plans are also coming out for individual sectors, providing some indication of how the government will prioritize and focus state resources under this policy. Examples include smart cars and logistics, including a stated goal of building 200 e-commerce pilots in cities nationwide and growing e-commerce trade volume by $3.7 trillion by 2016.

The Xi government is also increasing its political capacity to deliver on these objectives by centralizing power over IT and internet technology policy. In March MIIT announced that the government will set up a leading small group for strengthening national manufacturing to advance implementation of the Made in China 2025 plan. Together with the Central Network Security and Informatization Leading Small Group this manufacturing group will help streamline policy support for technology development, overcoming bureaucratic fragmentation.

Over 150 outside technology and industry specialists provided input on the Made in China 2025 plan over a two and a half year drafting process, lending more credibility to the plan's content. Beijing is also looking to outside experts at universities such as Tsinghua and state research institutes such as the Chinese Academy of Sciences and China Academy of Engineering for strategic input on the Internet Plus Strategy.

While the main beneficiaries of the plan will be Chinese companies with increased regulatory and localization risks for foreign firms, Beijing will also seek to lower formal barriers for foreign investment where domestic technology levels are weak. The main risks to US firms will be more "soft discrimination," intense competition from Chinese firms, and stricter security reviews. When the national security law, counterterrorism law, and cybersecurity law are passed there will also be added compliance costs and risks to core IP.

U.S. firms will still have opportunities in China market as formal barriers to entry in technology sectors comes down

Counter to the conventional view, the government does not want to fully prohibit foreign firms from the IT market, and, in fact, is taking steps to create new market opportunities for foreign technology firms in sectors like e-commerce and value-added services for telecom. This underscores a basic recognition in Beijing that foreign technology will be needed to support economic restructuring and industrial development goals as the economy shifts to a model of more efficient and sustainable growth. Beijing's aim is also to gain reciprocal market access for Chinese technology companies in global markets.

Moreover, foreign firms will not lose market share at the pace and to the degree that some fear because the government will have difficulty with implementation. Financial IT systems are highly complex and integrated, creating significant cost and technological burdens for Chinese banks. Domestic IT suppliers will lag behind foreign counterparts in technological capabilities for the foreseeable future, particularly when it comes to data security. Bureaucratic fragmentation will also be an impediment; MIIT, CBRC, and the Ministry of Finance are each responsible for different aspects of banking information systems. Lack of full consensus among Chinese users who recognize local options are not the most secure will also impede implementation.

Even the Made in China 2025 plan and Internet Plus Strategies will open new opportunities to US companies despite being targeted primarily at boosting China's domestic industry. The Made in China Plan specifically encourages more joint research and development (R&D) and overseas mergers and acquisitions (M&A) to gain access to foreign expertise and capital especially where indigenous capabilities are weak.

But the costs to U.S. firms of market access are rising

Even as these formal barriers to market entry come down, the costs of market access in these sectors will increase. Recent state support measures in technology sectors such as cloud computing and integrated circuits will primarily benefit domestic firms, increasing competition for market share and driving down prices as the technology gap shrinks. Competition from Chinese companies that have acquired IP from foreign partners will also intensify. Data localization requirements will add costs associated with building new data centers. US firms will have to weigh the benefits of market access with added local data storage requirements, IP risks surrounding new licensing approvals, and security reviews especially in online data transmission.

Recommendations for US policymakers

Beijing is likely to be less receptive to pressure from US officials than in the past given the current policy climate. Reports that Beijing had backed down on the counterterrorism law following a conversation between President Obama and President Xi proved unfounded. As a result US industry and policymakers will need to take a more proactive approach and be forward-looking in navigating increasing risks in China's policy environment.

As a result, it will be important for US companies to have space for maneuverability regarding the extent of the enforcement when these policies and directives are finalized. The US government should seek dialogue with Beijing with the goal of having the final regulatory language be broad and discretionary, rather than provoking Beijing to dig in deeper and leave US companies with limited options for operating in China's market. US companies will benefit from having a spectrum when it comes to implementation.

US policymakers and regulators should convey to the Chinese government the ways in which a their hardline approach undermines core objectives of President Xi's economic policy agenda – and how such policies can hinder Chinese companies as well as foreign companies. Selecting technology suppliers based on localization rather than market competition around the most secure systems will expose Chinese government and financial institution networks to security risks. Added compliance costs on Chinese technology companies will weigh especially on emerging technology start-ups at a time when Beijing is seeking to promote innovative small and medium sized companies. Data localization laws will hurt Chinese companies seeking foreign investment by restricting their ability to export information about credit. US policymakers should also focus on areas of leverage such as access to US markets for Chinese companies.

There is also a growing risk that these disputes set a negative tone for ongoing negotiations of the US-China Bilateral Investment Treaty (BIT). China's unwillingness to cede on new IT policies and national security exemptions could impede progress, especially if US companies continue to face market access problems related to technology transfer and localization requirements. The non-discriminatory treatment provision of the BIT would be helpful to US companies on these issues, but Beijing does appear willing to apply this provision to the IT sector despite pressure from the Obama administration as negotiations on the negative list move ahead this year.

The US government should also work with international partners to come up a common set of best practices and guidelines. Countries with more cooperative trade relationships with China such as Germany or Japan could send a powerful message to Beijing working alongside US stakeholders.

PANEL I QUESTION AND ANSWER

COMMISSIONER WESSEL: Thank you, both. Very helpful testimony on what is clearly a critical issue and growing in importance, I think, not declining.

Mr. Schruers, Section 301 of the trade law allows private parties, and I believe the association you work for qualifies under the definition of interested party. Why don't you bring a 301 action if the government is not doing enough?

MR. SCHRUERS: Well, I appreciate that. I think it's--we've sort of faced this question in a number of situations. Generally my answer is Internet censorship is not very effectively resolved in a government-to-business context. This is a government-to-government issue.

COMMISSIONER WESSEL: But a 301 would get the U.S. government to be the party that goes to the Chinese, not business-to-government.

MR. SCHRUERS: Yes. And we've been public that we have discussed with the U.S. Trade Representative the framework and possibilities of making trade disputes in various contexts. The fact is I think we need to have a certain degree of commitment from the U.S. government to proceed along those lines.

And so I think that's always a possibility, and it's not a possibility that we'd necessarily rule out, but it isn't something either that a trade association is going to proceed with absent some indication from U.S. policymakers that there's a willingness to go forward.

COMMISSIONER WESSEL: I appreciate that, although that raises some troubling questions since I assume your association is one of the principal interlocutors with the U.S. government. The comment about the lack of commitment or certainty you might have seems to me to indicate that the effort to continue to try and resolve this between the U.S. and China at the dialogue level is going to continue despite the national importance.

And dialogue naming and shaming doesn't seem to have in any way delayed, deterred, or denied the Chinese from proceeding. Where do you think the greatest objections are within the U.S. government to pursuing this?

MR. SCHRUERS: Well, I don't want to speculate as to the non-public communications inside government agencies. I will acknowledge that bringing such a case would require buy-in from the U.S. Trade Representative as well as the relevant oversight committees, I imagine, in Congress, and, of course, such a case would be difficult--not legally difficult.

As I've stated, I think the legal grounds are quite clear. It would be somewhat more administratively complex because generally when you look at trade disputes that the United States has brought, for example, before the WTO, we see a case regarding a specific good or a specific service, and in the services context, it's often in a specific sort of mode of delivery in the GATS framework.

And what we're really talking about here is an entire means of delivery of services across the entire economy, and the impact of censorship and filtering has distinct and somewhat different impacts in multiple service areas. So it would be a more elaborate case that would need to be brought, and it would require a large quantity of resources to bring this, much more so than say the audio-visuals case that we did, which was more narrow.

And so I would say, I'll be the first to say I think the USTR works very hard with limited resources and that would be a large resource commitment.

COMMISSIONER WESSEL: And I, hopefully, this will be subject for a second round of questioning. But understanding that whether this goes to Article XXIII or a serious prejudice nullification and impairment, larger concepts rather than, as you point out, product specific, to me it seems we've reached the point where there are really few economic repercussions for the Chinese.

And the result is they'll continue down the current path until there is some action-forcing event, and to me the U.S. is leading this, but the Europeans and others, I think, have similar interests in trying to get these policies abated in China.

MR. SCHRUERS: I agree entirely.

COMMISSIONER WESSEL: Okay. Thank you.

HEARING CO-CHAIR GOODWIN: Commissioner Fiedler.

COMMISSIONER FIEDLER: A couple of points and a couple of questions. Censorship is not new to China. So U.S. Internet companies have been shall I say acceding to Chinese censorship for years. So it seems to me that the localization issue, not the censorship issue, is the one that you're most concerned about.

MR. SCHRUERS: I think there's two issues there, and both are sort of valid concerns. Mandating or so-called forced localization is a more recent development that has evolved as the Chinese policies on Internet content have evolved, and it has a number of consequences, many of which are trade related and problematic.

COMMISSIONER FIEDLER: Let me put it another way. The Chinese are more sophisticated now in their ability to conduct censorship.

MR. SCHRUERS: Yes.

COMMISSIONER FIEDLER: Is that the big difference? Before when U.S. Internet companies didn't particularly care about individuals getting censored, now I have a hard time believing that they all of a sudden care about censorship. It seems to me that it's localization, getting forced out of the market, that is the concern here, not so much--and using the excuse of censorship, which they have seized on, and so you're seizing on it.

The issue of foreign technology. You, Ms. Sacks, said, and we hear this all the time, and I'll criticize you for the same thing I criticize other witnesses, we think that we can tell the Chinese what's in their interests, i.e., your infrastructure is going to be at risk if you do this, as if they're stupid, which I'm unwilling to accept that they're stupid.

They have demonstrated lots of smarts on many different levels. So I don't think that's a winning argument with the Chinese, and, by the way, on another level, I want their infrastructure to be vulnerable, as we'll hear today how vulnerable our infrastructure is.

So in the end, to me, I don't want to oversimplify this, but it comes down to their decision on national security. I think that the localization issue is a byproduct to their desire to maintain control, not just social control. Social control doesn't give the full picture. It's political control. It's control of the country, okay, that they're afraid of, and technology weakens their control of the country.

We have all said for years and years the Internet is the great democratizer. Guess not. It's showing itself to be a weak democratizer. So this is really a national security issue, and if we want to make it an issue, the WTO trade cases don't seem to be the way to do it--too slow--that retaliation in some form is what is called for here. I.e., why are we letting them raise money in the U.S. capital markets? How would you retaliate? I mean just off the record.

[Laughter.]

COMMISSIONER FIEDLER: Since you don't seem to be willing to talk about things outside of the sort of the--I mean just like expand on what--actually maybe Ms. Sacks is a better person to ask how to retaliate because you won't answer.

MS. SACKS: I'm not going to offer specific information about retaliation, but I will say that this is absolutely an area of leverage that we have to focus in on our strategy, but I won't--I can't comment on specific retaliation.

COMMISSIONER FIEDLER: The problem I have is that we think in a legalistic framework, and they don't, and they're operating with abandon, and we're sitting here letting them raise money on the capital markets. We're enabling the system you're criticizing, and nobody is thinking about retaliation. What? Americans just sit there and take it?

MS. SACKS: I wouldn't think of it as retaliation so much as points of leverage, and I think our strategy has to acknowledge that we have leverage, and this is a two-way street, and this is absolutely part of Beijing's--

COMMISSIONER FIEDLER: How do you demonstrate leverage other than using it? I mean they don't obviously believe that we have leverage because we're not using any. You have to use some in order for people to understand that you have it.

MR. SCHRUERS: If I may, the WTO framework, although I acknowledge that it is slow, has been proven to work in other contexts. I think there was--some success can be attributed in the audio-visuals case.

COMMISSIONER FIEDLER: I submit to you not where they perceive an overwhelming national security issue. I don't think it's succeeded in any country where that country has believed that their national security is at stake.

MR. SCHRUERS: Certainly national security interests do come into the calculus, and I don't disagree with the contention that Internet censorship in China is often founded on at least some measure of some view that there is a national security reason to do that.

But let me take a step back and just say our complaints here are principally founded on a failure to comply with the rule of law, and if we do not utilize the international rule of law framework that the United States has largely been responsible for constructing, then we very much undermine the legitimacy of our own legal arguments, and the WTO does provide for retaliation, and if we want to retaliate and if we want other countries to retaliate, that is possible when a state fails to comply with a WTO ruling. And so in many ways bringing a WTO case opens up opportunities for other nations to more or less pile on and support the objective of the U.S. foreign policy.

COMMISSIONER FIEDLER: After the market has been wiped out for you probably, like the WTO and other trade cases do to domestic companies in the United States, where they act after that market, those companies have been destroyed. It's a timing problem. I'm seriously concerned about effectiveness in the end.

HEARING CO-CHAIR GOODWIN: We'll see if Commissioner Reinsch can coax more off-the-record statements out of you.

[Laughter.]

CHAIRMAN REINSCH: Well, the first comment I would make is just following up Commissioner Wessel's comments. I have known Ed Black, who I think is still your boss, for 35 years. He has never been reluctant to pursue a confrontational strategy, in my experience. Never. So if he's not pursuing one this time, I can only assume it's because other people are reluctant to follow, and I think we've got a good sense from your comments where that reluctance likely is, and that's very useful.

Let me pursue for a minute the WTO strategy that you outlined. Supposing the U.S. government does go to the WTO with the kind of case you're talking about. Suppose we win. What do we get?

COMMISSIONER FIEDLER: Nothing.

MR. SCHRUERS: Well, so I mean we've won WTO cases in the past, including against China. Generally speaking, a panel decision and ultimately an appellate decision, should there be one, will prescribe or will indicate remedies. The parties often negotiate over the remedies.

And if there is a failure to comply, the winning party can be authorized to take retaliatory measures.

CHAIRMAN REINSCH: Let's be a little more specific though. In this case, you will know what we're alleging because it would be, in effect, your case. What do you think the likely remedy would be that the WTO would dictate? That they stop doing what?

MR. SCHRUERS: I can imagine a number of remedies. I think certainly discontinuing arbitrary and unannounced filtering and blocking of content would be one. Providing some sort of regulatory transparent mechanism whereby parties would know when and if content is going to be blocked which may itself be an opportunity for further consultation since a lot of the blocking that we're seeing is overbroad.

CHAIRMAN REINSCH: Okay. Let's just take those two for the moment. Let's say that we have a case; we win. The WTO tells them they need to do that. Okay. And then they don't or they don't to our satisfaction. Retaliation is authorized. What kind of retaliation would be feasible in a case like that?

MR. SCHRUERS: Well--

CHAIRMAN REINSCH: It's not that we would exactly do the same thing to them.

MR. SCHRUERS: No, and indeed often the retaliatory measures that are authorized aren't in the same sector or mode of service that is affected. Recall that in the WTO case involving online gambling, the Antiguan authorities--

CHAIRMAN REINSCH: Right.

MR. SCHRUERS: --retaliated with respect to U.S. intellectual property, in part because that was perceived, I think accurately, by Antiguan authorities as the strongest point of pressure on the United States. So in many ways, the retaliatory measures can be tailored to the political interests of the losing party and may be effective for precisely that reason.

Now, I'm really not in a position to speculate as what that will be at some point in the future.

CHAIRMAN REINSCH: Sure. But you guys as the presumed instigators of all this or your other association colleagues could spend a lot of time and a large pile of money because you're going to have to hire lawyers and economists, et cetera, et cetera, et cetera, things that some of us here thrive on, in order to win.

HEARING CO-CHAIR GOODWIN: There's nothing wrong with hiring lawyers.
[Laughter.]

CHAIRMAN REINSCH: I'm not going to respond to that.
[Laughter.]

CHAIRMAN REINSCH: And so you win, and then you discover that somebody else gets the prize and not you. Isn't that kind of a deterrent to going forward?

MR. SCHRUERS: Well, I guess, would sort of disagree with the implied statement that the gains of retaliatory measures are the sort of a prize. In the long run, the Internet and technology firms want an open competitive market, and ultimately the retaliatory measures are merely a means to an end, and that end is a free, open and competitive Internet.

CHAIRMAN REINSCH: Okay. I understand that. Are you or actually either of you familiar with the Green Dam U.S. litigation case?

MR. SCHRUERS: I'm not--I am familiar with the case, but I'm not familiar with the specifics or the posture, and so I can't comment specifically on--

CHAIRMAN REINSCH: That's too bad because I was going to ask you how it turned out, but--

MR. SCHRUERS: So my understanding is that, which again may be incomplete, is that that was largely resolved through informal consultation. I don't know to the extent that we actually proceeded with a formal dispute.

CHAIRMAN REINSCH: No, I'm not referring to what the Chinese did. I'm referring to litigation in California over theft of code from an American company.

MR. SCHRUERS: Oh.

CHAIRMAN REINSCH: And I'm getting to this because this is a tool that I think has been inadequately used by other companies.

MR. SCHRUERS: Yes. Well, I mean let me say I'm sorry, I misunderstood what we were talking about. Insofar as there is a misappropriation or infringement claim, that is attractive in these computer intrusion scenarios where information is taken, and the information taken is subject to either state or intellectual property rights. But that's actually a very narrow subset of what we're talking about here.

In a lot of cases, intrusions result in information being extracted which is not really IP subject matter, and in other cases we're really not talking about intrusion at all, but rather just simply blocking somebody from access to the market, which doesn't really implicate intellectual property concerns.

CHAIRMAN REINSCH: So that would be a tool with limited applicability?

MR. SCHRUERS: It is. As an IP lawyer, who is also very happy to be hired, I think intellectual property is very valuable in the area where it's relevant, but a lot of what we're talking about here is not that area.

CHAIRMAN REINSCH: Okay. I've got one for Ms. Sacks, but I'll defer to later. Thank you.

HEARING CO-CHAIR GOODWIN: Chairman Shea.

VICE CHAIRMAN SHEA: Well, thank you both for very interesting testimony.

I'm going to follow up a little bit, I think, on Commissioner Fiedler's point. I agree with him that the idea of telling the Chinese what's in their self-interest is kind of fruitless because they have a keen sense of their own self-interest, and I hear fewer and fewer public officials in the United States talking about training the Chinese to see their own self-interests. They rarely, rarely say that anymore today.

But, Ms. Sacks, you had a statement, which I think Commissioner Fiedler jumped on. You mentioned it again in your oral statement. You said U.S. policymakers should also focus on areas of leverage such as access to U.S. markets for Chinese companies.

Now we're a policymaking group here. We advise the Congress. What, could you just flesh that out? Help us focus on areas of leverage such as access to U.S. markets for Chinese companies. What do you mean there? Flesh that out if you don't mind.

MS. SACKS: There's a high-level strategy in Beijing to promote Chinese companies abroad, and there's been a focus in particular on Chinese companies that are in value-add high technology sectors.

VICE CHAIRMAN SHEA: Uh-huh.

MS. SACKS: So we know that this is a point of political priority that we do have leverage. I'm not a policy advocate or even analyst so I can only look at what I observe. So you all have a much more difficult job than I do--

VICE CHAIRMAN SHEA: Right.

MS. SACKS: --in actually coming up with solutions to these questions. I can just say that this is a point of political attention right now in Beijing that was made very clear in the Made in China 2025 strategy. So if you want to get a sense of where those points and leverage are, I would look at the types of sectors that the government has prioritized for national expansion.

VICE CHAIRMAN SHEA: Uh-huh.

MS. SACKS: Know that =there could be some movement.

VICE CHAIRMAN SHEA: Okay. So you're basically saying they want things too. They have interests too, and we could exploit those interests to, as points of leverage to change their behavior.

MS. SACKS: With an emphasis on reciprocity and that this is a two-way street.

VICE CHAIRMAN SHEA: Okay. Reciprocity. I'm glad you brought that word up. Reciprocity. I think it's not a dirty word, but a lot of people think it just doesn't make too much sense, I think reciprocity can make sense in certain circumstances. So tell us about reciprocity. What's your vision? What do you mean by reciprocity? What's your definition?

MS. SACKS: This is about access to markets in China and outside of China.

VICE CHAIRMAN SHEA: So if we don't get access to your market, you don't get access to our market; is that what you're saying?

MS. SACKS: I don't know how I would say it in such quid pro quo language, but I think that there is certainly an understanding of that in China, and I think that in the last year, we have seen an effort by the Chinese government to lower formal barriers to market entry in a number of a sectors, and we can have a separate discussion on how far-reaching those efforts have been and whether they go far enough, but I think that that effort is driven in part by this notion of reciprocity, and that's why we've seen a revised foreign investment law under draft right now. That's why we're seeing a move towards the negative lists for foreign direct investment in China.

In Beijing's thinking I think that reciprocity is absolutely a part of the calculation for these shifts.

VICE CHAIRMAN SHEA: Okay. So I'm a little confused. So I don't see the United States engaging in reciprocity as a tool of leverage, a leverage point, to gain access to Chinese markets. So you're saying that the Chinese are responding to U.S. pressure on reciprocity or--

MS. SACKS: No, I'm saying that this idea of reciprocity has been an important driver in China's own efforts to revise its foreign direct investment regime for attracting inward investment, that there is an understanding that if they continue to keep formal barriers to markets high, that that will influence the calculation in the United States--

VICE CHAIRMAN SHEA: Ah.

MS. SACKS: --in terms of their access to our markets, and that has been an important driver in their thinking on their own inward foreign direct investment.

VICE CHAIRMAN SHEA: So they're changing these laws as a precautionary measure to prevent people, policymakers in the United States, who may take a more aggressive stance from acting on that desire to close markets or impose economic--

MS. SACKS: It's something that they can point to show, look, we're doing something on this front. I mean even in the last few months, you can see now e-commerce firms are allowed to own 100 percent of shares in China's market. Value-added services in the telecom market, there have been reductions in the restrictions there. These are things that the Chinese government can point to as examples as they're looking to gain access to markets abroad.

VICE CHAIRMAN SHEA: Okay. Thank you.

HEARING CO-CHAIR GOODWIN: Commissioner Tobin.

COMMISSIONER TOBIN: I have lots of questions. I want to take advantage of both of your areas of expertise to understand operationally how this works in China.

Let me start by saying when we were briefed, we were informed about the new regulations that the Chinese government is pursuing. For example, the number of government approved products made by the U.S. network equipment maker Cisco Systems fell from 60 in 2012 to zero in 2014. Ciscois a premiere U.S. corporation,one of our country's best. How does it work when one's on the list and then not on the list? Do they keep whatever computer products of that maker in place?Or does everything end/sunset in a few years?

And since, at least, Ms. Sacks, you counsel firms, what choices does Cisco have, given that policy? Are they going to be forced to work, orpartner with Chinese companies? Have you ever seen a company that says no, I won't encrypt orlet you have access to the encryption formula? So if you would, please inform me on how it works for a stellar company like Cisco?

MS. SACKS: Right. Thank for your question.

The government procurement lists are one of the tools that the government is using right now to increase its oversight and control over foreign technology, but I should say that in the government and the financial sectors, we think that there will be the most severe restrictions in the near term, but that doesn't mean the entire market.

And so I think that for U.S. firms, they need to understand that selling to government and banking buyers is going to be much more restrictive, but private sector purchasers, it's going to be a little bit different, and so I would focus on other types of end users in the private sector.

There's a strategy right now in place for small and medium-sized enterprises in China. There's going to be a tremendous amount of growth for SMEs. So the extent to which they can focus on their sales on those areas and partnering with Chinese firms is going to be very important. It's going to be particularly important to decide who those partners are, particularly now as the anti-corruption campaign is expanding. There's been some discussion that potentially that's tapering. We don't think that that's the case. It's more important than ever to assess and backstop those relationships.

Chinese firms that are in sectors that have been prioritized for support under the Made in China plan, under the Internet Plus strategy, are going to be in an advantageous position so it's important to align with those kinds of government support priorities.

But at the same time, they also need to be aware of the regulatory risks that are increasing. So I'm not saying it's going to be easy, but it's about looking for those specific windows of opportunity.

COMMISSIONER TOBIN: So are they, in effect--interesting word here-- rerouting themselves, a company like Cisco and others, and is that what is going on?

MS. SACKS: I think absolutely that U.S. tech firms now have to adjust their strategies to account for this new political reality. Localization is something that's been talked about for years, and we're seeing more political capacity and commitment to actually deliver on that in a way that's fundamentally changing the landscape.

COMMISSIONER TOBIN: Thank you.

Mr. Schruers, and you have many other companies you're working with.

MR. SCHRUERS: Yes, which I'll be clear does not include Cisco, but since you mentioned them specifically, I think certainly nations can reasonably have sort of procurement specifications, and I think that what we see, at least in the international trade context, is a requirement that those be administered in a transparent and open fashion and where decisions are explained with some process and procedure and may be appealable.

So you know I don't think the question is so much whether or not this choice should have been made but whether or not it was made with a process that U.S. service providers and hardware providers can contest. And certainly a lot of the decisions similar to the Cisco story that you mentioned are a function of sort of recent disclosures about U.S. intelligence community practices, which I think it can be fairly said have had a broad negative impact on U.S. trade in both exports and services.

COMMISSIONER TOBIN: Thank you.

HEARING CO-CHAIR GOODWIN: Let me play devil's advocate and see if I can get a little bit more detail and perhaps context about the proposed counterterrorism and national security laws. I mean obviously we look at these proposals and say they're protectionist in nature, they're going to hurt Western investors and especially American companies.

The Chinese undoubtedly respond by saying we're acting in our own sovereign interests and in our national security, and point to recent revelations over the past couple of years of what they would characterize as comparable American security actions taken by NSA and the Brits with regard to cyber intrusions and so forth.

So the question for me is what's the contrast? What are the differences between their proposed laws and the requirements for localization and access to encryption codes and so forth? Contrast that with our own protections for our national security when it comes to investment by tech firms, including, of course, Huawei, which we've made it virtually impossible for them to operate here in the United States.

MS. SACKS: I'll start with the national security law. There have been some comparisons made between the national security law and a national security review regime that would be set up as a part of it and to the U.S. CFIUS process, and I would argue that that comparison is not exactly accurate because the way that the national security law has been put forward suggests that it will be far more broad and all encompassing in its scope, allowing a legal justification for restricting investment on the basis of national security because that particular transaction would, it would impact social stability, ideology, all areas of the economy, prosperity. I mean the list goes on. It's not national security as narrowly tailored as I think that our process would be.

So for that reason it's somewhat more worrisome. There's also been a provision of the law that calls for cyber sovereignty, which again would provide a legal basis for Beijing's ability to have further controls over Internet content.

So this is going to be far more reaching in scope. We've already seen some national security review bodies set up in the four free trade zones that are in China, and it will be important to watch how those national security review bodies go forward in the next year as an indication of Beijing's thinking on the role that they will play in the investment climate as well as their conceptualization of national security.

In terms of the counterterrorism law, it's still too early to get a sense of specifically what this is going to look like. I think that the language again is going to be broad, which is going to be helpful to U.S. firms, as I've mentioned before, because there's going to be a spectrum when it comes to implementation, you know, encryption access, data localization. There should be room for maneuverability as far as how that actually is implemented, and that's a good thing when it comes to our perspective, but it's a little too early to make a comparison yet on that front.

I'm not sure if you want to add any other comments.

MR. SCHRUERS: I wouldn't add a whole lot to that actually, only that, of course, with the specific matter of procurement in the United States, when the U.S. procures hardware, we do so pursuant to open specifications. There is an appeals process, which as we well know can sometimes drag on for some time. Procurement decisions can be heavily contested in the United States, and that's a good thing. That is process that ensures that a decision is fact-based and not politically oriented.

The sort of choices that we're seeing in China don't always necessarily comport with that. And, of course, when it comes to sort of censoring and blocking of content, if iTunes suddenly goes down because athletes are buying a Tibetan charity album in the run-up to the Olympics, that's not something that has any comparable counterpart in the United States, and so there's really no equivalency there whatsoever.

HEARING CO-CHAIR GOODWIN: Thank you.

In a second round, Commissioner Wessel.

COMMISSIONER WESSEL: Thank you both again.

Ms. Sacks, let me see if I understand you and correct me quickly if I'm overstating this. To sum up your comments, I sort of hear you say "get over it," get over what China is doing and find a way to navigate the waters. And your organization does a great job in advising clients about that, that we are not going to get the kind of systemic change that we might want so find those targets of opportunity, and they exist. Is that an accurate, fair summation?

MS. SACKS: I don't know if I would say "get over it."

[Laughter.]

MS. SACKS: In those words. I think that we just have to recognize that this is the operating environment right now, and that we are at a time in which the Chinese government is going to be less likely to cede to U.S. pressure or international pressure than perhaps they have in the past, and I think there's also an understanding that from the perspective of U.S. industry, these companies need to play in the China market.

So I'm not naive about the risks associated with that market, but I think for companies that are there and have a significant amount at stake in those markets, the most productive thing we can do is focus on where there are windows of opportunity.

COMMISSIONER WESSEL: And from a business perspective or from the analytical side, I accept that. I don't mean to fault you in that sense. But from a governmental policy perspective, what I hear from what you're saying is, we're not really going to change China. Again, find the best ways to navigate that. But from a public policy perspective, it seems that we then are going down a slippery slope where more code, more JVs, a lot of other things that happen over time, and at some point, you reach the point of no return where there is such an invested interest by our companies in the China market in not tipping the cart over that we have no leverage, we have no interest.

And to go to the earlier discussion about where the problem is in terms of getting action with China, I'd argue to you, yes, there's some flaws in our own governmental objectives and desire to take this on, the will. I think there's also a real problem with our business community, that sort of the old adage they want others to bloody their nose while they hold the coats.

So are we at risk of getting past a tipping point that you're going to help companies navigate upstream as the headwaters get slimmer and slimmer and the fruits get slimmer and slimmer? Too many cliches. I apologize.

MS. SACKS: No, it's a good question, and I think that--and again, I'm not in the government so my job is not to think of policy solutions.

COMMISSIONER WESSEL: But you were in the government. Okay.

MS. SACKS: Much, much more difficult position than I am, and I was an analyst just observing these trends from the outside. Again, not making policy decisions. So I can only say I think that my concern is that we don't want to provoke Beijing into taking a more hardline stance and digging in deeper on these issues. The worst outcome, in my mind, would be a counterterrorism law is approved, and the language is so narrowly tailored that then U.S. firms have no room for maneuverability; right? And so that's not a scenario that we want either.

I think that the U.S. government also needs to make sure that we're really invested in our own technology innovation because at the end of the day our companies' ability to compete in China, localization policies or not, is going to be about our technical edge.

That's the difference. When I sit back and I look at sectors in which I see more space for U.S. firms than others, it comes down to where we have an edge competitively or not. So we have to maintain our technological edge. Otherwise there's absolutely no hope. So can we focus on that?

And I also think that the internal debates that we have here in the U.S. over things like encryption access, over the relationship between the national security community and Silicon Valley, those internal debates, and a lack of unity and consensus on that, is further weakening our bargaining position with the Chinese government, who not only see us as hypocrites coming out of the Snowden era, but now see us as not being in a place where we have, we understand the answers to those questions on our own shores. So these are things that I would focus on.

COMMISSIONER WESSEL: Thank you.

HEARING CO-CHAIR GOODWIN: Chairman Reinsch.

CHAIRMAN REINSCH: Just following that up a little bit, Working with companies, I can see the dilemma they face, and I understand your position is to advise the companies and help them achieve their objectives. You're not a policymaker.

But have you ever had a situation in this area with respect to China where you've simply advised companies that the juice isn't worth the squeeze and they should get out?

MS. SACKS: So part of being a political risk analyst means sometimes giving bad news, and I think particularly at Eurasia Group, we pride ourselves on being objective. We're not invested in a particular outcome. So at the end of the day, if we weigh multiple scenarios, we're not going to necessarily say this is absolutely what you should do, but what we will do is we'll go through and look at different scenarios, and it will become very apparent in looking at those scenarios sometimes that something may not be the best outcome or the best path to go down.

CHAIRMAN REINSCH: Is departure one of the scenarios that you regularly analyze?

MS. SACKS: That one actually is not something that--well, it is an option that I have considered, that we consider among other options.

CHAIRMAN REINSCH: Well, right, I wasn't suggesting it was the only one.

MS. SACKS: Yeah.

CHAIRMAN REINSCH: But it's not generally one that you look at?

MS. SACKS: It is one among others.

CHAIRMAN REINSCH: When you were alluding to "bright spots" in your testimony, you referred to continuing Chinese statements that they welcome R&D and investment in R&D, which I assume is joint R&D. I mean that's what they would be primarily looking for.

MS. SACKS: Yes.

CHAIRMAN REINSCH: How do we maintain the technology edge that you just referred to through joint R&D programs?

MS. SACKS: I think some of that technological edge has to do with R&D that happens here, far away from China. Companies absolutely go into the China market understanding that there are IP risks associated with joint R&D and oftentimes elect not to bring over their frontline next generation techniques and products to the China market.

And I think that there's also an understanding that China is actually getting better when it comes to innovation. I don't know if people could say this a few years ago. Under the Hu Jintao Administration, there was a lot of emphasis on innovation, not a lot to show for that, but that's changing now. And there's a lot of innovation going on in China.

CHAIRMAN REINSCH: In my experience in my day job with my members, which are mostly big companies, they tend to fall into three categories. The first are the ones that I think Commissioner Wessel believes includes all of them, which is that they're making money, and so they're not interested in rocking the boat, no matter how many holes the boat might have in it.

The second group may or may not be making money but believes that they are adequately protecting their IP from various incursions.

And the third are the people that have serious grievances and decide either to leave or to fight.

I want to pursue The second group for just a minute. I've had a number of companies say that they believe they've taken adequate steps, either by keeping their IP here or taking whatever protections they think are appropriate. My observation is that in almost every case they're wrong about that. Have you found companies that have been or who have told you the same thing, and are you in a position of making a judgment as to whether they're right or not?

I mean have you found companies that are actively engaged in R&D in China and marketing in China who have been able to protect their intellectual property from the kinds of incursions that we're talking about?

MS. SACKS: Yeah. I mean I would tend to agree with you. I think that a lot of the time people are not as aware as they should be of the extent to which their IP is at risk in these joint ventures, in the joint R&D projects, despite thinking otherwise.

CHAIRMAN REINSCH: Well, that would be something that you as an expert would be in a better position to at least have an opinion about when you consult with them. I mean is that one of the topics that companies ask you to look into?

MS. SACKS: Absolutely.

CHAIRMAN REINSCH: And I assume there are other firms that look at quality of security devices, and they look at their hardware and software and make judgments about whether it's adequate, which I assume is not what you do?

MS. SACKS: I do not do that, no.

CHAIRMAN REINSCH: Okay. I'll stop there. Thank you.

HEARING CO-CHAIR GOODWIN: Commissioner Fiedler.

COMMISSIONER FIEDLER: A couple things. I'm going to play off of one of your answers, Ms. Sacks, to Mr. Shea on reciprocity. You used an example, you said--I mean it's the exchange about whether it was leverage, whether the Chinese were anticipating that we might do something. The example you gave was an e-commerce company--e-commerce, meaning, as far as I understand you're communicating buy-sell decisions and actions, not anything particularly politically sensitive.

So it splits the business community, i.e., the e-commerce company is okay, but the Internet provider or the Googles of the world are not okay because I mean how do you censor an e-commerce transaction?

On the question of capital markets, the Chinese are opening their capital markets, and the expectation is--haven't fully opened it yet, but have opened it up to institutional investors in a much bigger way than they have in the past and are planning to in the future. It seems to me we may have missed that train, i.e., that they are going to be less interested in our capital markets, and that theirs will adequately suffice because they're going to attract the international capital to their exchanges.

Mr. Reinsch was getting at, and I think he asked the question, can you protect intellectual property at all? I mean he said that some people think they can. We're going to hear this afternoon, I think, that you can't protect anything via the Internet.

If you have Internet access, if your intellectual property is accessible through the Internet, it's gone, which is the bigger issue here, it seems to me, overall, which is a national security issue, a cyber. I'm not unsympathetic with the Chinese actually, and I mean this very carefully, in that they've made a decision on what their national security interest is, and they've gone about and are doing it, I would say, quite effectively.

The argument is are we defending our national security interests effectively? I think we're going to get into that this afternoon. But your members are sort of collateral damage to the national security issues that exist between the United States and China. Is that a fair characterization?

MS. SACKS: Absolutely. On the latter point, I think that the challenge is that the U.S. government has a two-front battle right now. One is an internal one, and it's about regaining the support and trust of the U.S. tech industry, but the second one is the ripple effects of that and how that's perceived abroad.

And the problem is--and most recently, you know, Secretary of Defense Ash Carter announced his new cybersecurity strategy as part of a tour in Silicon Valley. The message that is perceived on the Chinese side is that there's even closer relationship between our government and industry at a time in which there's already mistrust and there's problems as far as export trust. Okay.

COMMISSIONER FIEDLER: Or when push comes to shove, our companies will do the right thing.

MS. SACKS: Right.

COMMISSIONER FIEDLER: That is a different--there's a significant difference there, and I would hope that when push comes to shove, our companies do the right thing.

I want to get into the question of need--I think you mentioned need the market. What do you mean "they need the market"? They don't need the market. They need the market if they want to make much, much more money. They don't need the market to make money. They need the market to make more than they could otherwise. That's different. That's a choice.

Banks don't lend to poor people--okay--on the scale that they might otherwise because the risks they perceive are too great. Internet companies seem to be going to China despite the risks that they are encountering. And now, and what galls me frankly is that they were silent during the Internet censorship of people, workers, students, writers, people that generally go to jail, and now you want my sympathy for the market. And I'm sort of like playing hard to get on that question.

MR. SCHRUERS: May I? I'm happy to offer an answer to that. One technical matter, earlier on, you mentioned that e-commerce doesn't necessarily implicate national security, but I could think of a number of examples of e-commerce transactions, physical or digital audio-visual works that contain culturally sensitive materials, for example, as just one of many examples.

But that's more for the record. More to your question about whether or not Internet companies have been raising this concern, you know, in my capacity working for the association for over ten years, this has been an issue that is one of the chief issues that I've worked on. I or other representatives of my organization or other representatives of our industry have appeared before numerous committees, commissions, and agencies in the federal government for, going back, in my personal recollection, at least seven or eight years, raising these concerns and talking about how these trade issues.

COMMISSIONER FIEDLER: Let me put a finer point on it. They went into the market understanding that they would have a lot of their stuff stolen, and that their software stolen, this, that and the other thing stolen, and they tolerated a certain level of theft. Then the theft became grand theft, and they don't want to tolerate it anymore. That's my experience sitting on this Commission for almost a decade now.

MR. SCHRUERS: So as an intellectual property lawyer, I think intellectual property is great. It puts bread on my table, right, so I'm a big fan and proponent of intellectual property. A lot of the problems that we're talking about in the censorship context are not intellectual property issues. A lot of the reasons why U.S. services are exiting the Chinese market do not have to do with intellectual property.

I recognize that there is a subset of issues that are intellectual property issues involving forced disclosure of source code or loss of trade secrets through joint ventures, but that is an entirely separate set of issues from the sort of blocking and filtering and censorship and forced localization that I discussed in my own comments and that are discussed extensively by the NGOs and U.S. agencies that are pointed to in our testimony.

So IP is an issue. There are a lot of issues here that are not IP issues, and the concerns that are being raised are not about loss of intellectual property but are about inability to access the market through services which largely are not providing IP-centric services.

COMMISSIONER FIEDLER: I have more for a third round unless you want to give it to me now.

MS. SACKS: I just wanted to add, to answer your first question about going back to the reciprocity point and e-commerce. I think this is exactly why we're seeing a more difficult environment right now for negotiation of the U.S.-China BIT, and it gets to this point about

China's negative lists and what are they going to be willing--the idea that national treatment for foreign companies really is going to depend on the extent to which Beijing is willing to move on that negative list, and I think that's going to be one of the most difficult points in negotiating a U.S.-China BIT related to the ICT sector.

COMMISSIONER FIEDLER: I think you may be right. I also think--and you do political risk analysis--the willingness of the Chinese to push the envelope on a, at multiple levels is at a high, and I think it's a function of the centralization of power of Xi Jinping.

And you mentioned earlier in passing that you don't think the anti-corruption campaign is over. I don't want to change the subject, but one could make the argument--I actually do make the argument that all of what we're talking about in terms of localization is probably a national security domestic security decision.

One problem of wording here is we don't generally, when we talk about national security, we don't generally only mean domestic security. Okay. When they say national security, national security includes the survival of the Communist Party. Okay. We're not talking about the survival of the Republican Party or the Democratic Party. So their decisions are much more consequential in their own belief, i.e., they think that they're a little more fragile than anybody else in the world thinks.

And so these decisions, unless there is some sort of, in my view, extralegal pushback that changes the equation that they have, you're not going to see a solution to your localization problem.

Their perception of the United States of not pushing back, whether it be the South China Sea, whether it be here--and I think we are actually pushing back more in the South China Sea than we have in the past--but pushing back here, I think their read over the last 20 years is that we are perhaps more interested in money than we are in national security. That probably is about to change in light of the recent cyber intrusions that are sort of like over the top.

I mean one must give them credit. It's brilliant from a counterintelligence point of view. I mean if you want to dump millions of names of people and their backgrounds, that's pretty smart. I hope we're doing the same thing.

But it's a different environment, and I don't see where business--business always in a heightened national security environment loses. Even in the United States, national security trumps business. So I don't see this getting resolved in business' favor any time soon as it escalates in a national security world.

MS. SACKS: And this again is one of the fundamental differences in the Chinese context, that business is a part of national security, and that the Party's legitimacy is not just based on social stability in terms of mass protests. It's also based on perceptions of prosperity, and the extent to which people perceive the Party as enabling prosperity, that becomes a national security issue.

COMMISSIONER FIEDLER: That's right. That's right. And they do, employment is a higher priority than it is in the United States.

Thank you.

HEARING CO-CHAIR GOODWIN: Commissioner Slane.

COMMISSIONER SLANE: Thank you for coming, and I've been fascinated by this conversation.

My question is do you advise your clients that if they threaten the stability of the Chinese Communist Party, they will be crushed?

MS. SACKS: I advise my clients to align their business strategy in China with the priorities of the Chinese government and the Party. So to the extent to which they can demonstrate a commitment to Xi Jinping's reform agenda to national security, the way that they can align with that and show that they are supportive of it will lead to more success in the China market by giving them an avenue to get buy-in from stakeholders within the Chinese government. And from their Chinese partners, they need to present--they need to show the ways in which they are allowing their Chinese partners to also demonstrate those commitments to the Chinese government priorities.

COMMISSIONER SLANE: Thank you.

HEARING CO-CHAIR GOODWIN: Commissioner Wessel.

COMMISSIONER WESSEL: Thank you.

Ms. Sacks, you've opened up another line of questioning, and I'm not sure you're going to want to answer so I'll give you that caveat up front.

When Congress was urged by the business community and the administration to approve PNTR, which actually helped lead to the creation of this Commission, one of the comments was that engagement with China would lead to change. What I just heard from you is you counsel companies to align themselves with the interests of the Chinese leaders, with the understanding not to make waves, try and make money. How, from a public policy standpoint, should--and we advise Congress, who has broader interests or different interests, shall we say, than the business community--how should we take that?

You know we have probably a BIT coming up at some point, which raises numerous questions. Last week the President indicated, which I don't think will happen any time soon, that if TPP were to pass, that China has shown an interest in being a participant.

If we policymakers want to try and effect IP protection, greater democracy, freedom, et cetera, but the business community is seeking to align themselves with the interests of the Chinese Communist Party, isn't that at odds?

MS. SACKS: Let me give you an example of the kind of objectives that I've outlined very recently, and these are very broad. They are things like job creation. They are things like promoting the environmental agenda and energy efficiency.

COMMISSIONER WESSEL: This is for companies doing business here?

MS. SACKS: No. This is for U.S. companies to do business in China.

COMMISSIONER WESSEL: I was being facetious.

MS. SACKS: Okay. These are very high-level goals that I think there's common ground on. Technology innovation. There is space I think for cooperation there. On climate change. On helping inland remote areas have access to broadband and higher-speed telecommunication services.

I don't think these are problematic at all, and, in fact, I think that it serves both entities to be promoting these types of goals.

COMMISSIONER WESSEL: And I agree with that, but when it comes to other goals such as Internet freedom, greater accountability in the workplace for the right to organize, bargain collectively, et cetera, it seems that U.S. companies operating in the China market stand back because that is making waves.

Certainly helping a U.S. company that promotes energy efficiency would be embraced in China--for good reasons. But on areas where U.S. policy interests may not converge with China, it seems that U.S. companies are not only not agents of change, they are often an impediment here to trying to have more aggressive policies to promote change.

MS. SACKS: Well, some of those areas are outside the scope. As I mentioned,

I'm focused on the list that I described before. I'm not going to get into whether I advise--I don't advise my companies on issues related to Internet censorship. That's outside of the line of sectors that I tend to focus on. So I don't really know how--yeah.

COMMISSIONER WESSEL: But every company doing business there from a manufacturing entity,--

MS. SACKS: Right.

COMMISSIONER WESSEL: -- has some interest in those issues. What I hear you saying--

MS. SACKS: Right.

COMMISSIONER WESSEL: --is, again, don't make waves. If you're going to be in China, recognize the climate, and know that to succeed you have to play along. Don't try and promote change in other ways. Again, very different than what we heard when PNTR was being argued, that U.S. companies would actually help promote the kind of engagement, the kind of democratization that we haven't seen.

MS. SACKS: Democratization is not really in my scope here, but I think that also on manufacturing, there are a lot of ways in which U.S. manufacturing companies are far ahead of Chinese companies when it comes to things like labor standards, conditions for workers, and rights. Now I actually think that the Chinese government is under a lot of pressure from its own people to try to improve working conditions, and so the ways in which my clients are able to help them further those goals in the manufacturing sector is absolutely something we'll focus on.

Please don't distort the way that I'm talking about this.

COMMISSIONER WESSEL: No, I'm not trying to distort. I'm just saying that the business and policy interests are divergent in many areas here, and we have companies now that find that their activities in China have not yielding all the profits they would like. Certainly, as Mr. Fiedler pointed out, they are gaining, they are certainly reaping profits, but in the IP area, they want their government to do more, but they often don't step up to back that up, and that's a real concern.

Mr. Schruers, do you want to--

MR. SCHRUERS: I wanted to add, there's been a number of examples of U.S. service providers that have noisily exited the Chinese market.

COMMISSIONER WESSEL: Agreed. Agreed.

MR. SCHRUERS: And in doing so, you know, I regret to say they were applauded, and the testimony that I submit quotes, I think, from a very effective editorial saying why are U.S. policymakers applauding U.S. services exiting the Chinese market instead of trying to back them up with the tools that we have in international law to open those markets? Right.

Instead of applauding their departure, we should be decrying our own policy failures and trying to ensure that they can stay in the market. I can provide other examples. I don't want to name particular names here or call on a particular business. But there's a lot of cases of U.S. services exiting the market and trying to provide services into China from abroad and, quite frankly, other countries that restrict to ensure that citizens there can obtain the information that they're lawfully entitled to obtain.

So I don't think it's fair to say that the U.S. business community hasn't stepped up. There's been a number of cases where online services have sacrificed a potentially lucrative market because they were unwilling to comply with the constraints that were being imposed on them.

COMMISSIONER WESSEL: And I agree with you on both counts. Number one, I do applaud those who have left on principle. I also believe, as you do, that our government hasn't done nearly enough. I'd prefer that they stay there as well and that the climate change.

MR. SCHRUERS: Right.

HEARING CO-CHAIR GOODWIN: Chairman Shea.

VICE CHAIRMAN SHEA: I just have a question of fact. You mentioned the indigenous innovation catalogs. This is not precisely on topic, but it was raised earlier. The government procurement catalogs that required indigenous innovation. It's often said that these catalogs upset the EU, Japan, the United States, and there was a multilateral pushback on indigenous innovation, and that has been cited as a success.

I've also heard that, yeah, the central government got rid of the catalogs or the indigenous innovation requirements in them, but provincial catalogs are heavily laden with that, and even at the central level its kind of guidance is not provided in written form; it's just sort of a wink and a nod and verbal communication.

Do you have any views on this?

MR. SCHRUERS: I can't comment on specific details, but I am aware that this is a concern, and I think insofar as there are formal or informal or unspoken rules to favor domestic production, that's certainly a problem. It's a problem that we have the tools to resolve, and I think it's a legitimate issue for U.S. policymakers to attempt to confront.

I think there are other experts on the subject who can speak more specifically to where precisely those are arising.

VICE CHAIRMAN SHEA: Okay.

MR. SCHRUERS: But insofar as they are an issue that we need to confront, we do have some tools for that.

VICE CHAIRMAN SHEA: Ms. Sacks, do you have any views?

MS. SACKS: The way that indigenous innovation is often understood here in the U.S. and in the West is somewhat of a mischaracterization of the term, and I think that there are even greater threats from an IP perspective than people might realize.

If you look at Chinese science and technology policy, the term "indigenous innovation" specifically refers to acquiring and assimilating foreign technology, innovating on it and making it your own. And I think it's important to understand this as the context; this is the operating environment. And this is not new. We're talking about an environment of heightened risks. This definition of indigenous innovation goes back years.

VICE CHAIRMAN SHEA: Yeah. Okay. Thank you.

HEARING CO-CHAIR GOODWIN: Commissioner Fiedler.

COMMISSIONER FIEDLER: A quick question on cloud computing, just a factual one: how many U.S. companies soliciting U.S. customers are storing stuff on the cloud in China? What percentage of the market do you think?

MR. SCHRUERS: I'm afraid I don't have that information.

COMMISSIONER FIEDLER: It exists though, right?

MR. SCHRUERS: There are some. I think it's safe to say that there are some services that are continuing to store data in country in part because that's probably mandated by local requirements.

So, for example, last I knew, I think certain cloud office services are sort of blocked because the data isn't stored locally, and that's often driven by law enforcement and security requirements. The cross-border provision of cloud office services, for example the office productivity services, is something that can be done remotely from country to country. There's obviously no technical reason why they need to be stored locally, and so barriers to that I think would constitute trade violations, provided there's a commitment.

COMMISSIONER FIEDLER: I understand the problem inside China, i.e., U.S. companies selling to, and having access to, Chinese customers, and the Chinese government saying we want access to that cloud.

MR. SCHRUERS: Right.

COMMISSIONER FIEDLER: What I was asking is the reverse actually, which is that I'd be more concerned about services that are selling to the U.S. customer--

MR. SCHRUERS: Oh.

COMMISSIONER FIEDLER: --and their cloud is there.

MR. SCHRUERS: That I can't answer, and certainly there's--

COMMISSIONER FIEDLER: So you would agree that if the Chinese government was demanding access to that cloud data, that would be a problem?

MR. SCHRUERS: Well, we have legal processes under which government and law enforcement authorities can demand access to information that is in their jurisdiction.

COMMISSIONER FIEDLER: We have warrants and--

MR. SCHRUERS: We have warrants and so on.

COMMISSIONER FIEDLER: We have warrants and they don't.

MR. SCHRUERS: Well, precisely how the domestic law enforcement mechanisms operate is sort of beyond my expertise, but provided there are processes; a nation can demand access to data in its jurisdiction only under appropriate circumstances.

COMMISSIONER FIEDLER: I understand that. I mean the question is different though if one of their requirements is that you give us a backdoor to your cloud.

MR. SCHRUERS: Indeed, yes. And that's a problem. And it's a problem when other governments do it as well, including ours.

COMMISSIONER FIEDLER: We're not other governments' commissions. We're the China Commission.

[Laughter.]

COMMISSIONER FIEDLER: So I'm only asking about China.

MR. SCHRUERS: Right.

COMMISSIONER FIEDLER: I think everybody in this room would be concerned if they had unfettered access to cloud data that originates in the United States with customers. Then they don't have to be working very hard to steal it.

HEARING CO-CHAIR GOODWIN: I want to thank the witnesses for their time this morning. We're actually running a little bit early so barring any objection from my fellow commissioners, we'll start back up at ten till 11 and take a short break right now.

Thank you.

PANEL II INTRODUCTION BY VICE CHAIRMAN DENNIS C. SHEA
HEARING CO-CHAIR

VICE CHAIRMAN SHEA: Our second panel will address the Chinese government's efforts to penetrate U.S. computer networks, particularly the espionage attacks that are aimed at obtaining commercially valuable information.

The attacks have been perpetrated by a variety of actors in China, from the People's Liberation Army to groups of hackers sponsored by the Chinese government and following Beijing's direction.

Paul Tiao of Hunton & Williams' Washington office represents the interests of U.S. companies doing business in China. He served as Senior Counselor for Cybersecurity and Technology to the Director of the FBI. He is a former Assistant U.S. Attorney in Maryland. He has taught cybersecurity law and policy at George Washington University and Northwestern University.

Welcome.

Our second witness is Dennis F. Poindexter who is the author of The Chinese Information War: Espionage, Cyberwar, Communications Control and Threats to United States Interests. He is also the author of The New Cyberwar, which will be published in September.

Mr. Poindexter has had a long career in the U.S. intelligence community and is a member of the President's Critical Infrastructure Protection Committee.

Thank you for being here.

And our third witness is Jen Weedon, who is the Manager of Strategic Analysis at Firefly--FireEye--excuse me--a computer security firm.

She and her team advise a range of government and private sector clientson cyber threats. Previously, as a manager at Mandiant, she was one of the authors of Mandiant's landmark report linking a long-running cyber espionage effort to a Chinese military unit.

So I want to thank all of you and apologize for my slip-up there on FireEye. So why don't we start. Remind all the witnesses just please keep your oral remarks to seven minutes, and we'll start with Mr. Tiao.

OPENING STATEMENT OF PAUL M. TIAO, PARTNER, HUNTON & WILLIAMS

MR. TIAO: Thank you.

Chairmen Shea and Goodwin and other members of the Commission, thank you very much for the opportunity to testify before you in this important hearing.

At Hunton & Williams, we represent energy, health care, financial, transportation, communications and other companies on cybersecurity preparedness, on incident response, investigations, litigation, and public policy issues. Many of our clients are the targets of the PRC government's commercial cyber espionage campaign.

So I commend the Commission for focusing on China's commercial cyber espionage threat. This threat presents one of the most significant economic and national security challenges facing the U.S.

As detailed in my written testimony, as well as the written testimony of my colleagues here at the panel, the Chinese government has engaged in a systematic program of commercial cyber espionage designed to advance the economic and industrial goals described in its 12th Five-Year Plan.

Consistent with these goals, the Chinese government through the People's Liberation Army, or PLA, has developed an extensive computer network operations program whose mission is to steal large volumes of valuable intellectual property, business sensitive information, and personal information from a wide range of U.S. companies with an emphasis on the industries prioritized in that plan.

Commonly described as an advanced persistent threat, the organized and persistent nature of the PLA's commercial espionage campaign complicates the network defense efforts of my clients and many other U.S. companies. PLA cyber actors share techniques among different hacking units. They continuously develop and improve on their malware tools, and they use highly sophisticated social engineering methods to compromise victim networks.

Recent data breaches involving the personal information held by two major health insurance companies, as well as the breach of federal employee data at the U.S. Office of Personnel Management, are widely believed to be attributable to Chinese hackers. If, in fact, that is the case, then the details about each affected individual's health care information and the information regarding background checks, security clearances, job assignments, job performance and the training of affected federal employees would provide Chinese hackers with a treasure trove of information for use in spear-phishing and other social engineering attacks.

The economic costs associated with the Chinese government's cyber espionage campaign takes on a variety of forms. As discussed in a study by McAfee and the Center for Strategic and International Studies and as borne out in our own work, such losses may include:

The loss of IP to a potential Chinese competitor that may be able to use it to develop and sell a competing product or to reduce R&D costs;

Reduced incentives for technological innovation by targeted companies;

The loss of confidential business-sensitive information that may, for example, be used by a Chinese company to underbid the victim for a lucrative contract or to undermine the victim's strategy in business negotiations;

Opportunity costs in the form of service and employment disruptions, lost sales and revenues, and reduced trust and use of online commercial activities;

The costs of securing networks, cyber insurance and recovery from cyber attacks;

Legal fees associated with breach-related litigation and government enforcement actions; and

Reputational harm suffered by victim companies and reduced stock prices.

The nature of these costs are illustrated in the ground-breaking indictment announced by the Department of Justice against five PLA hackers in May of 2014. That indictment details the ways in which the PLA used hacking methods to engage in commercial espionage for the benefit of Chinese industries and to the detriment of several U.S. companies.

In my own work representing corporations that are the targets of Chinese commercial cyber espionage, I witness firsthand the costs that they incur in order to prepare for and respond to cyber-based attacks.

For example, prior to an incident taking place, large companies devote extensive financial, staff and consultant resources to keeping information security policies up to date, implementing technical network security programs, developing and exercising breach response plans, participating in public-private and private-private cybersecurity information sharing arrangements, negotiating the information security terms of third-party vendor agreement, ensuring that those vendors maintain adequate information security, and purchasing cybersecurity insurance, and training employees.

If a significant cybersecurity incident takes place, then typically the CEO, the Chief Operating Officer, the Chief Information Officer, the Chief Information Security Officer, the General Counsel, the VP for Communications, the VP for Human Resources, and other senior executives work closely on a daily basis with lawyers from our firm and external digital forensic experts from companies like FireEye/Mandiant to oversee the response.

This would typically include an internal investigation of the breach and restoring the integrity of the network, engaging law enforcement if appropriate, developing and implementing internal and external communication strategies regarding that breach, analyzing the company's legal obligations, complying with state, federal and foreign notification requirements, complying with third-party contractual requirements, responding to inquiries from regulators, managing congressional inquiries, and defending against civil litigation and regulatory enforcement actions.

These measures, whether you're talking about pre-incident preparedness or post-incident response are very time consuming, they're expensive, and they can go on for years. So not surprisingly, the costs associated with data breach response and preparedness are on the rise.

So what can we as a country do to deter the Chinese government from engaging in commercial cyber espionage? The indictment of the five PLA hackers in May of 2014 could be helpful as it may introduce the possibility of jail time and restricted international travel into the minds of future would-be Chinese hackers.

However, the indictment has affected diplomatic relations between the U.S. and China and appears to have led to retaliation in different forms against U.S. companies doing business in China. It remains to be seen how frequently the Justice Department will seek similar indictments in the future.

The President's April 1, 2015 Executive Order on Blocking the Property of Certain Persons Engaging in Significant Malicious Cyber-Enabled Activities authorizes the government to impose financial sanctions on foreign hackers. In addition, the DOJ indictment of the PLA hackers provides a basis for the U.S. government to impose trade sanctions on the Chinese government or bring an action before the World Trade Organization.

However, it is unclear how often or in what way the new authority under the Executive Order will be used or whether the government will successfully pursue trade sanctions based on the DOJ indictment.

The enactment of cybersecurity information sharing legislation should assist private companies and the government in strengthening their network security, thereby making it more difficult for PLA hackers to conduct successful computer network operations.

Technical defense actions by private companies may in certain circumstances deter the PLA from attacking a company. However, instances of such forms of technical deterrence remain rare and not well understood.

So for all forms of deterrence, whether they are indictments, trade sanctions, economic sanctions against individuals or technical measures, we need to gain a better understanding of how they work and whether they are or could be effective. However, currently little analysis or effort is devoted to these questions. It is my hope that the government and the private sector can work together in the future to examine the effectiveness of different forms of deterrence and develop models of action that will someday persuade the Chinese government to reduce or end its campaign of commercial cyber espionage.

Thank you for the opportunity to testify.

PREPARED STATEMENT PAUL M. TIAO, PARTNER, HUNTON & WILLIAMS

Hearing on Commercial Cyber Espionage and Barriers to Digital Trade in China

June 15, 2015

Dirksen Senate Office Building Room 608
Washington, DC 20510

Paul M. Tiao
Partner, Hunton & Williams LLP
Testimony before the U.S. – China Economic and Security Review Commission

Chairman Reinsch, Vice-Chairman Shea, and other Members of the U.S. – China Economic and Security Review Commission, thank you very much for the opportunity to appear today to testify at this important hearing. My name is Paul Tiao. I am a Partner at Hunton & Williams LLP, where I am a member of the firm's Global Privacy and Cybersecurity Practice and Co-Chair of the firm's multi-disciplinary Energy Sector Security Team. I advise energy, healthcare, financial, transportation, communications and other companies on cyber and physical security preparedness, incident response, statutory and regulatory compliance, investigations, law enforcement, litigation, and public policy issues. Prior to joining Hunton & Williams in 2013, I served in the federal government for fifteen years as Senior Counselor for Cybersecurity and Technology to the Director of the Federal Bureau of Investigation, Judiciary Committee Counsel to the Assistant Majority Leader in the U.S. Senate, Assistant U.S. Attorney in the District of Maryland, and Trial Attorney at the Department of Justice. I am an adjunct professor of cybersecurity law and policy at George Washington University, and an instructor at the National Institute for Trial Advocacy. I currently serve on the Virginia Cybersecurity Commission, which was established by Governor Terry McAuliffe last year.

I commend the Commission for focusing on China's commercial cyber espionage threat. This threat presents one of the most significant economic and national security challenges facing the U.S. As discussed below, the nature of this threat has been documented in detail in recent private and government publications, the cost to U.S. industry is significant and growing, and the need for effective deterrent action by the government and the private sector is urgent.

As documented in reports published by leading network security and digital forensic investigative companies, reports issued from the federal government, statements by the President and senior public officials, and indictments announced by the U.S. Department of Justice, the Chinese government has engaged in a systematic program of commercial cyber espionage designed to advance the economic and industrial goals described in its 12th Five-year Plan. Issued in 2011, China's 12th Five-year Plan prioritizes growth in certain industries, including nuclear, wind and solar energy, energy conservation and environmental protection, drugs and medical devices, rare earth and high-end semi-conductors, information technology, aerospace, telecommunications, and clean energy vehicles.[1] According to the U.S. government, "Chinese leaders consider the first two decades of the 21st century to be a window of strategic opportunity

---

[1] KPMG, *China's 12th Five-Year Plan: Overview* (Mar. 2011).

for their country to focus on economic growth, independent innovation, scientific and technical advancement, and growth of the renewable energy sector."[2] Consistent with these goals, the Chinese government, through the People's Liberation Army (PLA), has developed an extensive computer network operations program that is systematically stealing vast stores of intellectual property, business sensitive information, and personal information from U.S. companies in these and other economic sectors.[3] Targeting these technologies and business information enables China's domestic companies to rapidly make "leap frog" technical developments and develop from favorable positions in business negotiations, thus expediting their growth into global market leaders.[4] The PLA's cyber command – housed in the PLA General Staff Department (3rd Department) – is estimated to have more than 100,000 personnel divided among 12 bureaus, three research institutes, and 16 regional and functional bureaus.[5] As detailed by Mandiant in a 2013 report featuring just one of those bureaus, a single PLA hacking unit was responsible for the theft of hundreds of terabytes of data from at least 141 organizations (115 of which are based in the U.S.) representing 20 major industries between 2006 and 2013, with the emphasis on industries prioritized in the 12th Five-year Plan.[6]

Commonly described as an Advanced Persistent Threat, the PLA's method of attacking a target company typically includes the following stages: 1) initial reconnaissance for the purpose of collecting information about the target company and its network environment; 2) initial compromise of the target's network, often through the use of spear phishing, strategic web compromises, and other social engineering tactics; 3) establishment of a foothold that ensures control of the target's network from outside of the network; 4) a cycle of privilege escalation that is designed to give the hacker expanded access within the network, internal reconnaissance of the target's network, lateral movement of the hacker within the network, and actions to ensure continued, long-term control over key systems in the network; and 5) completion of the mission through exfiltration of the desired data to the Chinese government via a series of compromised computers ("hop points") in the U.S. and around the world.[7]

The organized nature of the PLA's commercial espionage campaign complicates network defense efforts for U.S. companies, as PLA actors share techniques among different hacking units, and continuously develop, modify and improve on their malware tools.[8] In addition, the social engineering methods used by the PLA to compromise victim networks have become increasingly difficult to stop as hackers have become more sophisticated and corporate executives increasingly reveal details about their personal and professional lives on social media sites. For example, PLA hackers often leverage current or upcoming industry conferences in

---

[2] Office of the National Counterintelligence Executive, *Foreign Spies Stealing U.S. Economic Secrets in Cyberspace* (Oct. 2011).
[3] Northrup Grumman, *Occupying the Information High Ground: Chinese Capabilities for Computer Network Operations and Cyber Espionage (prepared for the U.S. – China Economic and Security Review Commission)* (Mar. 2012); Mandiant, *APT1: Exposing One of China's Cyber Espionage Units* (Feb. 2013) (hereinafter, "Mandiant 2013 APT1 Report").
[4] CrowdStrike, *Global Threat Intel Report* (2014).
[5] Mandiant 2013 APT1 Report.
[6] *Id.*
[7] Mandiant 2013 APT1 Report; CrowdStrike, *Global Threat Intel Report* (2014); Verizon, *2015 Data Breach Investigations Report*.
[8] CrowdStrike, *Global Threat Intel Report* (2014).

sending highly-tailored spear-phishing emails regarding specific topics to individuals who will likely attend the conference, or compromise the website devoted to that conference in order to infect individuals who visit that website with malware.[9] The recent data breaches involving personal information held by two major health insurance companies, as well as the breach of federal employee data held by the U.S. Office of Personnel Management are widely believed to be attributable to Chinese hackers.[10] If in fact that is the case, then the details about each affected individual's healthcare information and the information regarding the background checks, security clearances, job assignments, job performance and training of affected federal employees would provide Chinese actors with a treasure trove of information for use in spear phishing attacks.

The economic costs associated with the Chinese government's commercial cyber espionage campaign takes on a variety of forms, including the:
- Loss of intellectual property to a potential Chinese competitor that may be able to use it to develop and sell a competing product or reduce R&D costs;
- Reduced incentives for technological innovation by targeted companies;
- Loss of confidential business sensitive information that may, for example, be used by a Chinese company to underbid the victim for a lucrative contract or undermine the victim's strategy in business negotiations;
- Opportunity costs in the form of service and employment disruptions, lost sales and revenues, and reduced trust in and use of online commercial activities;
- Costs of securing networks, insurance and recovery from cyber attacks;
- Legal fees associated with breach-related litigation and government enforcement actions; and
- Reputational harm suffered by the victim company and reduced stock prices.[11]

The nature of these costs are illustrated in the ground-breaking indictment announced by the U.S. Department Justice against five PLA hackers in May 2014. The indictment details the ways in which the PLA used hacking methods to engage in commercial espionage for the benefit of Chinese industries and to the detriment of several U.S. companies, including Westinghouse, SolarWorld, U.S. Steel and Allegheny Technologies, Inc.[12]
- In 2010, while Westinghouse was building four power plants in China and negotiating other terms of the construction with a Chinese state-owned enterprise, including technology transfers, a PLA actor hacked into Westinghouse's networks and stole confidential and proprietary technical and design specifications for pipes, pipe supports, and pipe routings within the plant buildings.[13]
- In 2010 and 2011, while Westinghouse was exploring other business ventures with the same Chinese state-owned enterprise, the same PLA hacker stole sensitive, non-public,

---

[9] CrowdStrike, *Global Threat Report* (2013).

[10] Nicole Perlroth, David E. Sanger & Julie Hirschfield Davis, *Hackers tied to China amass trove of U.S. data; Breaches of government and health care firms expose files of millions*, NY Times (June 6, 2015).

[11] McAfee & Center for Strategic International Studies, *The Economic Impact of Cybercrime and Cyber Espionage* (July 2013).

[12] Indictment, U.S. v. Wang Dong et. al., No. 14-118 (W.D. Pa. May 1, 2014).

[13] *Id.*

and deliberative emails belonging to senior decision-makers responsible for Westinghouse's business relationship with that state-owned enterprise.[14]

- In 2012, at about the time that the U.S. Commerce Department found that Chinese solar products manufacturers had "dumped" products into U.S. markets at prices below fair value, a PLA hacker stole thousands of files including information about SolarWorld's cash flow, manufacturing metrics, production line information, costs, and privileged attorney-client communications relating to ongoing trade litigation. Such information would have enabled a Chinese competitor to target SolarWorld's business operations from a variety of angles.[15]

- In 2010, U.S. Steel was participating in trade litigation against Chinese steel companies, including one particular Chinese state-owned enterprise. Shortly before the scheduled release of a preliminary determination in one such case, a PLA hacker sent spear-phishing emails to U.S. Steel employees, some of whom were in a division associated with the litigation. Some of these emails resulted in the installation of malware on U.S. Steel computers. Three days later, the PLA hacker stole host names and descriptions of U.S. Steel computers , and thereafter took steps to identify and exploit vulnerable U.S. Steel computers.[16]

- In 2012, Allegheny Technologies, Inc., was engaged in a joint venture with a Chinese state-owned enterprise, and was involved in a trade dispute with that enterprise. In April of that year, a PLA hacker gained access to Allegheny's network and stole network credentials for virtually every Allegheny employee.[17]

In my own work representing corporations that are targets of Chinese commercial cyber espionage, I witness firsthand the costs they incur in order to prepare for and respond to cyber-based attacks. For example, prior to an cybersecurity incident taking place, large companies devote extensive financial, staff and consultant resources to keeping information security policies up-to-date, implementing technical network security programs, developing and exercising breach response plans, participating in public-private and private-private cybersecurity information-sharing arrangements, negotiating the information security terms of third party vendor agreements, ensuring that third party vendors maintain adequate information security, purchasing cybersecurity insurance, and training employees.

If a significant cybersecurity incident takes place, then typically the CEO, Chief Operating Officer, Chief Information Officer, Chief Information Security Officer, General Counsel, VP for Communications, VP for Human Resources, and other senior executives work closely on a daily basis with lawyers from Hunton and external digital forensic experts to oversee the response. This would typically include an internal investigation of the breach, restoring the integrity of the network, engaging law enforcement if appropriate, developing and implementing internal and external communications strategies, analyzing the company's legal obligations, complying with state, federal and foreign notification requirements, complying with third party contractual requirements, responding to inquiries from regulators, managing congressional inquiries, and defending against civil litigation and regulatory enforcement actions. These measures are very

---

[14] *Id.*
[15] *Id.*
[16] *Id.*
[17] *Id.*

time-consuming and expensive, and can go on for years. Not surprisingly, the costs associated with data breach response are on the rise.

So, what can we as a country do to deter the Chinese government from engaging in commercial cyber espionage? The indictment of the five PLA hackers in May 2014 could be helpful, as it may introduce the possibility of jail time and restricted international travel into the calculus of future would-be Chinese hackers. However, the indictment has affected diplomatic relations between the U.S. and China, and appears to have led to retaliation in different forms against U.S. companies doing business in China. It remains to be seen how frequently the Justice Department will seek similar indictments in the future.

The President's April 1, 2015 Executive Order on Blocking the Property of Certain Persons Engaging in Significant Malicious Cyber-Enabled Activities authorizes the government to impose financial sanctions on foreign hackers. In addition, the DOJ indictment of the PLA hackers provides a basis for the U.S. government to impose trade sanctions on the Chinese government or bring an action before the World Trade Organization. However, it is unclear how often or in what way the new authority under the Executive Order will be used, or whether the government will successfully pursue trade sanctions based on the DOJ indictment.

The enactment of cybersecurity information-sharing legislation would assist private companies and the government in strengthening their network security, thereby making it more difficult for PLA hackers to conduct successful computer network operations.

Actions by private companies that are the target of China's commercial cyber espionage may in certain circumstances deter the PLA from attacking a company. Recently, a network security firm announced that its proprietary monitoring technology had been used to identify PLA intrusion activity associated with zero-day vulnerability (a network vulnerability for which no official security patch has been issued). The firm reported this vulnerability to Microsoft, which then released a patch rendering the zero-day useless. Subsequently, the firm observed the same PLA hackers looking for the presence of the security firm's proprietary technology and withdrawing its intrusion efforts upon finding that technology.[18] Technologies with such capabilities are promising, but unfortunately examples of technical deterrence remain rare and not well understood.

For all forms of deterrence, whether they are indictments, trade sanctions, economic sanctions against individuals or technical measures, we need to gain a better understanding of how they may work and whether they are or could be effective. However, currently, little analysis or effort is devoted to these questions. It is my hope that the government and the private sector can work together in the future to examine the effectiveness of different forms of deterrence, and develop models of action that will someday persuade the Chinese government to reduce or end its campaign of commercial cyber espionage.

Thank you for the opportunity to testify today.

---

[18] http://blog.crowdstrike.com/cyber-deterrence-in-action-a-story-of-one-long-hurricane-panda-campaign/.

OPENING STATEMENT OF DENNIS F. POINDEXTER, AUTHOR OF THE CHINESE INFORMATION WAR, ESPIONAGE, CYBERWAR, COMMUNICATIONS CONTROL AND RELATED THREATS TO UNITED STATES INTERESTS, VIRGINIA

MR. POINDEXTER: Okay. I hope you read Andrew Browne's summary over the weekend of our problems with China recently. The first thing he said was President Nixon--this was in The Wall Street Journal. If you don't get The Wall Street Journal, then you probably didn't get it.

[Laughter.]

MR. POINDEXTER: What he said was--

VICE CHAIRMAN SHEA: The Washington Post. That's the Washington Post.

[Laughter.]

MR. POINDEXTER: Oh, yeah, well, okay.

[Laughter.]

MR. POINDEXTER: In his article--I've got to get back on track here again--he said in 1967 when Richard Nixon was trying to get China to join us, he thought Nixon was believing that China would be like us, and in the end, in his final statement, he said that Nixon said maybe we created a Frankenstein.

Now, I don't know about that part of it, but I do know about the computer security aspects, and China has a well-disciplined state architecture that is managed by the state with telecommunications companies that support central monitoring and censorship. They certainly know who's attacking us. Do we agree? Yeah.

We've seen China require monitoring tools like Green Dam on every computer made there. They require their Internet service providers to cooperate with monitoring and censorship. Over the past few years, we've come to accept that China is hacking a wide variety of industries and stealing both strategies and intellectual property. But they steal more than that.

When President Obama was running against Senator McCain, they hacked both of those offices, their leaders, and what China looks for there is they look for thought leaders. Who's going to give the President information and can we influence that person?

They aren't just hacking businesses. They've hacked industries that support our government and contractor personnel like, for example, the processors of security clearances, insurance companies, health care, defense industries, computer security companies, educational institutions and technology at all levels.

They steal teaming arrangements, pricing, competitive intelligence, and, most importantly, they take source code. They're even asking for it in China. Now what does that mean to us? Source code really has two purposes: one is you can use it to make object code, and you can sell it yourself; but the other is they can modify it, put it back in the system, and it looks just like the original except it does more than the original.

This is preparation for a new kind of war, and I tend to look at this from the information warfare standpoint. A popular Chinese author says it's a strategy of information war that uses three elements--psychological, media and information operations--to manage its enemies, and they're calling us one of those enemies.

The Chinese used attacks on The Washington Post, The New York Times, and Bloomberg teaming partners to dry up their sources in China. They're not content to just manage their own news; they want to manage ours.

We really hadn't been paying attention to what they're doing until five years ago when Google had problems in China. God bless Google. I'll tell you they're great when it comes to stuff like this. The do-no-evil guys were asked to filter some of their search results so certain things, like Falun Gong would be missing. They wanted them to take those out.

After escalating problems, China hacked Google, looking for dissidents on Gmail and some of that source code. After that, other security firms started getting in the game and looking for what China was doing. And they found a network called Ghostnet. You've probably been briefed on this. I think you know what it is. But Ghostnet was looking at the Dalai Lama. They hacked eight different embassies in different parts of the world finding out where his correspondence was, his letters, his own personal letters, and his plans. What good is that kind of information? You use it to head him off in what he's going to do in the future.

The Information Warfare Monitor published two reports. They were a year apart. And in the first report, they said we think it's China, but we're not sure because China is growing so fast on the Internet, we can't be sure of the communications. In the second report, which was in 2010, they said it definitely was China, and that's because attribution isn't so certain now as it has become since then in 2010.

We have business leaders who think they can out-innovate China no matter what they do, including some that have huge business operations there. We have whole industries that think they're capable of protecting their data from people who are intent upon taking it when they almost always turn out to be wrong, and they're competing with well-financed government operations, not other businesses.

We're not prepared to do that. Intelligence services and hackers have quite a bit in common, and we got into that in the first section as to what impact they can have on a business community. I thought it was great to listen to. The Chinese are perfectly willing to use stolen technologies to set up the competition for our business sectors. They use intelligence and military functions, university research centers, enhanced with state-owned businesses to gather information and apply it. Then they say we didn't do that; prove it.

That is the hacker defense. Anybody who has ever defended--this lawyer--a hacker in court knows that that is their defense. It wasn't me.

We can manage a range of devices on the Internet of Things that we can't trust, but we need to devise better ways to separate ourselves from it, keep foreign governments from using it against us while still allowing for us to use it as a communication and information medium.

The Chinese are good at all of those things. It takes a government and industry cooperation to be successful. We've got to get together in order to do it.

PREPARED STATEMENT OF DENNIS F. POINDEXTER, AUTHOR OF THE CHINESE INFORMATION WAR, ESPIONAGE, CYBERWAR, COMMUNICATIONS CONTROL AND RELATED THREATS TO UNITED STATES INTERESTS, VIRGINIA

Hearing date: 15 June 2015

Dennis F. Poindexter

Testimony before the U.S.-China Economic and Security Review Commission

Panel II, Commercial Cyber Espionage

A worker in a Chinese factory made a simple statement that got my attention. When she held up an iPad she was working on, and looked at the camera, she said, "Take care of this. We work hard to make it, and we want it to last a long time." I took better care of mine after that.

Most of the country believes the Chinese people are like us, and they are right about that. They are hard-working people, who work for less money than we do, make fantastic products that are popular in the world. But at that company, twenty of those workers had committed suicide the year before. The nets to stop others from doing the same thing were still up.

What we see most often is not the Chinese government. We are seldom reminded that China is one of the few Communist countries left in the world, and it is comfortable with that. We don't think about what that means very often. Their Army, Intelligence Services and senior government leaders are inseparable, centrally managed, and not very prone to criticism. In their government, it is wise to know how far a person can stretch his independence before making a leap.

We don't have an office of population control and could not imagine what that could be useful for. We don't have a censorship bureau either, but we contemplated one once during the Reagan Administration.

In China, there are many state-owned businesses (though a decreasing number). There is differing opinions about how successful the private sector is, and whether it is more successful.[1] The leaders send their sons and daughters to the best schools, most of them in the U.S. Spouses and relatives of ranking party members run some of those "private" businesses, and the Chinese have adapted their definition of "state-owned" to remove many companies that were once on that list. This Committee has heard testimony on the 88 Queensway group that operated several businesses out of the same address, and one of those was a front company for their Intelligence Services.[2]

Internet Service Providers have to sign agreements to support the efforts of the central government, and employ censors to help do that. Google did not particularly like having censorship rules applied to its global content and our news media are even less enamored with the idea.

---

[1] Nicholas R. Lardy, Markets over *Mao: The Rise of Private Business in China,* The Peterson Institute for International Economics, September 2014

[2] See Lee Lekowitz, Martella McLellan Ross and J.R. Warner, *The 88 Queensway Group: A Case Study in Chinese Investors' Operations in Angola and Beyond*, U.S.- China Economic and Security Review Commission, U.S. GPO, January 2011 & *National Security Implications of Investments and Products from the People's Republic of China in the Telecommunications Sector*, January 2011. Operations in Angola and Beyond, July 10, 2009

The Chinese see the Internet as something to be managed and controlled, where we see it as a vehicle for disseminating information and sharing communications and ideas. They have the well-known Great Firewall and Great Cannon, but the lesser-known *Golden Shield*. The latter is an interesting mix of a surveillance network that would combine the National, Regional and Local police and security agencies to monitor every citizen of China. They can match data against the new national ID cards carried by everyone.

If we combined the Federal agencies involved in national security, law enforcement, prisons, jails and border patrols, personnel management, traffic management, crime statistics, fugitive warrants, foreign affairs management, combined them with the Task Forces, state vehicle departments, and regional police, and linked in the local police forces, we might be able to have something close to what they were trying to build.

In 2009, China went so far as to require the installation of software called Green Dam in all computers made there. It would have allowed monitoring and manipulation of data on any computer made in China. The World Trade Organization finally ruled against them on trade grounds, but there are still 53 million PCs in China, with the software *voluntarily* installed.[3] They think big, and... they are not the same as we are.

If the Chinese have done half of the things attributed to them by cyber security companies, the Federal government, and private individuals like myself, they are the most active cyber thieves in the world. That characterization allows some to interpret what the Chinese are doing as solely criminal.

Over the past few years, we have come to accept that China is hacking a wide variety of industries and stealing both strategies and intellectual property, but they steal more than that.[4]

In President Obama's run against Senator McCain, the Chinese hacked both candidates and their staff for position papers and plans. They look for thought leaders in business, military, and governments and they monitor their positions over time. They are patient.

They aren't just hacking businesses. They have hacked industries that support our government and contractor personnel, like processors of security clearances, insurance companies, healthcare, defense, computer security, educational institutions, and information technology at all levels. They probably know more about our military, business, and government personnel than we do.

They steal teaming arrangements, pricing, and competitive intelligence. More importantly, they took source code, from commercial and government sites.[5]
Source code is the original that is used to make object code the computer can use. Source code is useful to them for two reasons: first, they can shortcut production by copying, selling and profiting from it: second, they can modify it for reentry into the system. It looks like the original, functions like it, and does more than the original. Neither of those is good for us.

We tend to think of this as crime, but this is not crime in the way we are used to. It is preparation for a new kind of war. A popular Chinese author says that this is a strategy of Information War that uses three

---

[3] Openet Initiative, *China's Green Dam: The Implications of government Control Encroaching on the Home PC*, https://opennet.net/chinas-green-dam-the-implications-government-control-encroaching-home-pc
[4] See *APT 1: Exposing One of China's Cyber Espionage Units* , APT 17: Hiding in Plain Sight: FireEye and Microsoft Expose Obfuscation Tactic and Operation for different perspectives on the extent of Chinese hacking. Mandiant is a FireEye Company.
[5] Examples are Avago, Google, American Superconductor Corp., Adobe, Cisco, U.S. Treasury Department

elements (warfares), psychological, media, and information operations, to manage its enemies.[6] One of those enemies is the U.S.

The Chinese used attacks on the Washington Post, New York Times, and Bloomberg teaming partners to dry up their sources in China. This year, they fired up their Great Cannon to blast companies serving up content like the Chinese language version of the New York Times. They apparently see something seriously wrong with the Times.

But the important thing is they are not content to manage only their own content; they want to manage ours. It gets harder to control as communications bypass governments and go directly from one person to another. Governments find it more difficult to track down any single individuals in millions of e-mails, Twitters, and postings on Facebook, but it is something they are capable of, given improvements in monitoring technology.

Cyberwar is partly the use of that technology. Intelligence Services and covert operations increasingly fight Cyberwars, but our military defined it. Colonel Liu Mingfu, in his book *The China Dream*, mentioned that word "covert" when describing the three types of warfare. Being covert is essential to plausible deniability. Governments know how this works.

Our military believes cyber weapons can make war and has described a broader concept of Information War since the late 1980's, exercising those principles by the early 1990's.[7] In our doctrine, this is Information War, though Cyberwar has begun to replace Information War as a term of reference. Part of Information War is Economic Warfare, where the Chinese seem to spend most of their time, doing admirable work.

They would argue that none of the things we see are war. In fact, China says it does none of them. We can say, in aggregate, they are attempts to manipulate us to accept their will. The Spratly Islands are the best example of current events that have been managed to allow China to achieve a political objective that few countries agree should have been successful. Hacking the countries around the South China Sea, lets them find out what the governments' positions might be, and influence them accordingly.[8] In the meantime, they built up the islands and armed them. They are good at managing perceptions, until it is too late.

There is some disagreement as to whether cyber weapons can be used to make war, regardless of their capabilities.[9] It is easy to understand those arguments, and call what our enemies are doing "cyber espionage", "monitoring", "economic competition", or another less sensitive word that does not imply a threat to our national security. It is easier to describe it that way, but not as accurate.

Leon Panetta recently left no doubt that disruption of our power grid or other types of direct attack against our infrastructure would be an act of war.[10] The Defense Department has described its response to cyber attacks as having the same potential for "use of force" as conventional attacks.[11] If cyber weapons are not war, we could not have a reason for war that stems from their use. Yet, the most difficult question to answer is not "Is it war?" but "Is a military response appropriate?" Cyberwar has changed considerably

---

[6] Bill Gertz, *Chinese Colonel on Information War*, The Washington Times, 4 June 2015
[7] Martin C. Libicki, *What is Information Warfare?* National Defense University, August 1995, page 1.
[8] Geok Meng Ong, Kenneth Geers, *APT 30: The Mechanics Behind a Decade Long Cyber Espionage*, FireEye Labs, 2015
[9] See Gal Beckerman, *Is Cyberwar Really War*, Boston Globe, 15 September 2013
[10] Jake Tapper, A Crippling Cyber Attack Would be an 'Act of War', This Week, ABC News, 27 May 2012
[11] Siobhan Gorman, *Cyber Combat: Act of War*, The Wall Street Journal, 31 May 2011

since these doctrines were published. The new version is more refined, subtle, and less oriented to military use.

We really hadn't been paying attention to what they were doing until five years ago, when Google reported some problems in China. The Do-No-Evil guys were asked to filter some of their search results so certain types of things, like the term Falun Gong, would be missing. There was a long list of other things. Google objected.

After escalating problems, China hacked Google looking for dissidents on Gmail, and some of that source code. After that, security companies and governments started looking for how they got in.

While the good guys were looking, they found something called *Ghostnet*, a China-based network used for hacking. This happens often in cyber operations and is testament to its current state. One of the targets was the Dalai Lama and the information being stolen was coming from eight country's embassies. They got 1500 of his personal letters. They got his intentions, his partners, and his plans. From that they can predict what he is going to do. China controls the distribution of ideas, modifies them to suit their own needs, removes them, or allows access to them and monitors those who have it. They manage thought leaders; sometimes with rewards for publishing what they want, other times by threats or jail. The free exchange of ideas is not free.

The Information Warfare Monitor et al, published two reports, a year apart[12] in the first one, they said it *might be* China; in the second, they said it *was* China who went after the Dalai Lama. This is because attribution has gotten better. Attribution, the ability to say with some certainty that is responsible for an event got considerably better after 2010. We are just now finding all the things that were done years ago.

We have whole industries that think they are capable of protecting their data from people intent upon taking it, when they almost always turn out to be wrong. They are competing with well-financed government operations, not other businesses. We are not well prepared to do that.

When Chinese hackers got into DoD's unclassified NIPRNET in 2007, the Defense Department downplayed it as a network carrying only unclassified information. If this type of data were not valuable, there would be no reason to have a costly network to put it on.[13] At the same time, the UK's Ministry of Defense was saying it was concerned about attacks against its Top Secret networks. [14] He added that these systems were not connected to the Internet. This belief that we can be separated from the Internet is common, but not practiced very well. We leak almost everywhere, yet business and government leaders swear they are secure.

If networks were static, we could say with certainty whether something was connected to the Internet and be sure that when we went back to check, a year from now, that it might not be true. In business, commercial network mapping was even more surprising, with some of our customers unknowingly having basic research accessible from the Internet, or committing financing to companies that were ill suited for operation in such a hostile environment. One large aggregation of networks had over 200 back-door connections. The Chinese have thousands of targets of opportunity, and they don't have the same trouble with their networks.

---

[12] Information Warfare Monitor, et.al, Shadows in the Cloud, 6 April 2010

[13] Robert Marquand and Ben Arnoldy, *China's hacking skills in spotlight*, Christian Science Monitor, 16 September 2007.

[14] Nick Hopkins, *Hackers have breached top secret MoD systems, cyber-security chief admits,* The Guardian, 3 May 2012

The Chinese manage a disciplined national architecture, using state-owned telecommunications companies to support centralized monitoring and manipulation of large quantities of data (Google-sized efforts). They prohibit Virtual Private Networks to expose any traffic to scrutiny.[15] That provides a safe haven for their operations. They can't say they don't know who is hacking us.

The Chinese are allowed to plow what they get - back into the economy. That part of the playing field is not level.

This is not a technical problem; it is a political one. We know who the Chinese are stealing from and how they are doing it. We know how they have made it more difficult for industries to operate in China. We know what industries they want to dominate and the consequences if they do. What we don't know is what to do about it.

The main difference between our political system and theirs is how we apply what we know. They are perfectly willing to use stolen technologies to set up competition for our business sectors. They use their Intelligence and military functions, university research centers, enhanced with state-owned businesses, to gather the information and apply it. Then, they deny everything, and say, "Prove it".

We can do better.

We have business leaders who think we can "out innovate" China no matter what they do. I'm not sure I want to bet on them being right.

We manage our health, reading materials, news, banking, home security, supply chains, travel, taxes, and a range of astounding new vehicles that may drive themselves on an Internet of Things – on an Internet that we can't trust. We need to devise better ways to separate ourselves from it, keep foreign governments from using it against us, while still allowing for us to use it as a communications and information medium.

Industry and government both have roles to play. They can focus much better together, than working on their own. Our own National Security depends upon that cooperation.

This statement has been approved for public release by the Office of the Director of National Intelligence. The views expressed in answers to questions are solely my own personal opinions, and not those of the Intelligence Community or United States Government.

---

[15] George Chen et.al. *China's Great Firewall Is Rising*, Foreign Policy, 3 February 2015

OPENING STATEMENT OF JEN WEEDON, MANAGER, THREAT INTELLIGENCE AND STRATEGIC ANALYSIS, FIREEYE AND MANDIANT, INC.

MS. WEEDON: All right. Thank you for the opportunity to testify.

My name is Jen Weedon, and I'm a Manager of Threat Intelligence at FireEye. FireEye provides software and products to help stop today's advanced cyber threats, and we have over 3,100 customers in 67 countries. Our Mandiant Consulting Services help companies investigate and recover from many of the high profile intrusions that you read about in the news.

Our Intelligence Team has been tracking the activities, tools, and targets of cyber threat actors globally. We've been looking at and tracking these guys for ten years now. Much of the malicious activity that we see hitting our clients in the commercial espionage space is from Chinese advanced persistent threat groups, and we define advanced persistent threat groups as essentially groups that have some level of state sponsorship and are able to tenaciously pursue their objectives at all costs.

Well-resourced advanced cyber threats that use sophisticated tactics are able to bypass conventional security deployments almost at will, and American companies are being forced to fight a battle against adversaries possessing nation-state capabilities, and this isn't a fair fight.

Based on our threat intelligence work over the past ten years, we believe the Chinese government largely uses cyber operations in three interrelated ways. One is to collect intelligence on other nations. The second is to conduct commercial espionage to enable and sustain economic growth, which is integrally related with the legitimacy of the Chinese Communist Party, and third is to maintain domestic control by strictly regulating and censoring the Internet.

Out of the dozens of advanced cyber threat groups that we track, by far the most prevalent and focused are those that are engaging in commercial cyber espionage.

Our experience and research has revealed several key lessons:

One is that nation state-backed groups are capable of circumventing even the best defenses because they're well-resourced and relentless;

Second, Chinese government-backed groups continue to engage in widespread commercial data theft at staggering rates, although their specific targets will start to change and evolve based on China's broader economic reorientation; and

Third, not all China-based groups are the same. They have different government sponsors, different targets, and varying degrees of state sponsorship or support. Some threat actors and groups that we track appear to be contractors. Certain individuals may moonlight on the side and operate for financial gain. In spite of these differences, though, the vast majority of China-based APT groups that we track are engaged in massive theft of IP from global corporations, particularly those involved in what the Chinese government views as areas of strategic importance.

The Chinese APT groups that we track don't choose their targets at random. We believe that there's both formal and informal tasking mechanisms between the threat group sponsors and the actors conducting the intrusions.

At a high level, China's strategic emerging industries act as an almost to-do list for China-based groups. No sector has gone untouched. We frequently see publicized data theft from defense organizations or government coffers. But there's a huge array of other sectors that have been hit. Just a handful of recent engagements or campaigns that we've tracked have been against the robotics industry, electronics, telecommunications, business application software, satellite communications, pharmaceuticals and everything in between.

In my written testimony, I included a table that maps all of the strategic emerging industries and the number of threat groups that we see active in those industries, industries like high-end equipment manufacturing. We've seen 22 separate groups of actors stealing information from these industries. Similar, with next generation IT. So this is a staggering problem.

As China's nearly 20-year period of rapid economic growth has slowed following the global financial crisis, there's been significant economic pressures, and China has prioritized rapid innovation and focused on stimulating domestic consumption, consumer spending, and services.

We think this reorientation will dramatically shift the targets that Chinese threat groups go after as part of their commercial cyber espionage program.

As China's efforts to spur innovation take on greater urgency because the economy is not growing fast enough or because there's unemployment, we see that they are already targeting organizations that are known for their innovation. This past May, our Mandiant Consulting Services aided Penn State in an investigation of Chinese hackers who have been so deeply imbedded in the computer network of the engineering college, they had to completely take it offline. This incident is not the exception. Even this past year alone, we've responded to two other cyber espionage incidents involving top U.S. schools engaged in very specific, sensitive, state-of-the-art R&D.

We think the APT actors will continue to target U.S. labs, university research institutions, and small businesses and start-ups because these organizations often lack the understanding of the risk or the resources with which to secure their environments.

Given the Chinese leadership's focus on understanding advancing entrepreneurship, we also believe they're pursuing information on the leadership, management, and organizational culture of highly innovative U.S. organizations.

In terms of some specific key commercial industries in the U.S. that we think they're going to target in the future, environment, energy and agriculture is a high priority. As the economy has grown and the environment has been degraded, the demands for energy, land and materials have outstripped available resources.

We know that food security is a major concern for Chinese leadership, and consequently we've already seen Chinese APT groups--one in particular targeted four separate companies involved in farming, agricultural chemical manufacturing, and agricultural equipment manufacturing.

Reliance on coal for electricity generation is obviously a major culprit of poor air quality and the shift to nuclear energy has prompted espionage targeting as well. The Chinese government came out and proclaimed they're going to take a series of nuclear safety initiatives. Not long after, several of our clients in this space were targeted by one of the most sophisticated groups we track, likely for data theft on these niche industries.

Future-oriented technologies, surveillance and big data are another top priority of the Chinese leadership. Manufacturing still remains one of China's key economic drivers, and clearly the Chinese leadership recognizes the potential of next-gen technologies. To that end, we've seen over 20 different groups target companies in the U.S. involved in these next-gen technologies.

One recent instance included the targeting of an electronics organization that specialized in law enforcement related surveillance technologies that probably support the government's push to better monitor their populace.

They've also set a goal of leading the world in the Internet of Things, earmarking almost a billion dollars of investment for 2015, and we've started to see some of our clients that operate in this space be targeted by these threat groups.

Health care and pharmaceuticals are something that are probably no stranger to you. It's been in the news a lot. The Chinese leadership is probably concerned about a series of major demographic shifts with increasing obesity, cancer villages, general sort of hypertension rates, and so this is all adding an urgency to the health care problem, and we've seen more than eight separate groups pursue victims in the pharmaceutical and health care industries, successfully targeting business strategic plans and goals, as well as information from human resources and legal departments, as well as specific cutting-edge research and intellectual property related to critical health challenges.

As one example, last summer we saw a campaign by one group targeting several oncology-focused biotechnology companies.

There is also the targeting of personal data. Intellectual property and business information is by far the most often stolen and sought after type of information from these groups, but it appears that within the last couple of years, particularly within the last year, some advanced cyber threat groups have stolen significant amounts of personal data from several different organizations.

The motivations for stealing this type of information are not yet entirely clear. It's possible that this interest in personally identifiable information is ultimately for monetary gain or criminal purposes, as we know that some of these groups operate as contractors.

Another working hypothesis is that the stolen information could be used to enable broader espionage purposes to better facilitate follow-on activity by identifying specific individuals, to better facilitate HUMINT recruitment, to make more effective social engineering campaigns and everything in between.

I've gone one minute over. So in conclusion, China-based cyber espionage actors will likely continue to target these industries in the U.S., but with a slightly different shift as their economic orientation determines what the most important information is that the Chinese leadership is seeking.

Thank you.

PREPARED STATEMENT OF JEN WEEDON, MANAGER, THREAT INTELLIGENCE AND STRATEGIC ANALYSIS, FIREEYE AND MANDIANT, INC.

June 15, 2015

Jen Weedon

Manager, Threat Intelligence

FireEye, Inc.

Testimony before the U.S.-China Economic and Security Review Commission

Hearing on Commercial Cyber Espionage and Barriers to Digital Trade in China

Introduction

Thank you for the opportunity to testify. My name is Jen Weedon, and I am a Manager of Threat Intelligence at FireEye, Inc. FireEye provides software to stop today's advanced cyber threats, serving 3,100 customers in 67 countries. FireEye's Mandiant Consulting Services helps companies investigate and recover from intrusions and shore up their security programs.

Our Intelligence Team tracks the activities, tools, and targets of cyber threat actors globally, including groups we assess to be state-sponsored, financially motivated cyber criminals, or hacktivists. Much of the malicious activity that we see hitting our clients is from Advanced Persistent Threat (APT) groups. APT actors generally have some level of government sponsorship or support, persistently pursue their objectives, and are capable of using a full spectrum of tactics, techniques, and procedures ("TTPs) to conduct data theft and/or disrupt, deny, degrade, or destroy networks. One of our most publicized reports on an APT group was the APT1 report, which describes APT1's multi-year, enterprise-scale computer espionage campaign in detail and links APT1 to China's 2nd Bureau of the People's Liberation Army (PLA) General Staff Department's 3rd Department (Unit 61398).

In our current environment, this type of state-sponsored cyber activity is a common tactic that nations use to gain advantage over one another. Well-resourced advanced cyber threats that use sophisticated TTPs are able to bypass conventional security deployments almost at-will. American companies are being forced to fight a battle against adversaries possessing nation-state capabilities, which is not a fair fight.

A successful cyber operation has the potential to significantly benefit a threat sponsor, and the magnitude of data theft we see is of virtually unquantifiable economic, political, and military value. Advanced cyber threats often emanate from countries that not only refuse to hold attackers accountable for their crimes but also provide resources and direction. Accordingly, there is very little risk and relatively few costs for them, given the enormous imbalance between the resources necessary to defend a network and the resources necessary to attack one. Cyberspace is an asymmetrical domain, where a single attacker can generate work for hundreds, if not thousands, of defenders.

Based on our threat intelligence work over the past 10 years, FireEye believes that the Chinese government largely uses cyber operations for three interrelated purposes: 1) to collect intelligence on other nations, 2) to conduct commercial espionage to enable and sustain economic growth, and 3) to maintain domestic control by strictly regulating and censoring the Internet. Out of the dozens of advanced cyber threat groups we track, the more than 20 China-based groups we watch are by far the most focused on commercial and political espionage.

Our experience and research has also revealed several key lessons:

First, nation state-backed groups are capable of circumventing even the best defenses, because they are well-resourced and relentless in pursuit of their goals.

Second, Chinese government-based cyber espionage groups continue to engage in wide-scale commercial data theft at staggering rates, although their specific targets will likely evolve over time based on China's broader economic reorientation.

Third, not all Chinese threat groups that FireEye tracks are the same. They can have different government sponsors, different targets, and varying degrees of state-sponsorship or support. In addition, some threat actors and groups appear to be contractors. Certain groups and individuals moonlight on the side and conduct operations for financial gain. In spite of these differences, though, the vast majority of China-based advanced threat groups are engaged in massive theft of intellectual property from global corporations, particularly those involved in what the Chinese government views as areas of strategic importance.

Chinese Commercial Cyber Espionage Driven By National Priorities; Groups Relentless in their Pursuits

China's commercial cyber espionage activity likely supports Communist Party central planning policies designed to provide a competitive advantage for Chinese companies. This is a coordinated approach that pits government-backed Chinese enterprises against foreign firms in a race for innovation and economic dominance, often with detrimental effects for U.S. companies.[1]

The strategic importance of this economic espionage means that the actors are both well-resourced and relentless in their pursuit of a corporation's proprietary data. If one of these advanced threats targets a company, a security breach is inevitable. This even applies to companies with robust and mature cyber defenses. In 2014, FireEye conducted hundreds of investigations in 13 countries, and during these investigations, we found approximately 10 new pieces of malware per work-hour that had successfully bypassed the defenses of security-conscious organizations.

Chinese APT groups do not choose their commercial targets at random. FireEye's research and analysis indicates that there are probably both formal and informal tasking mechanisms between groups' sponsors and the actors conducting the intrusions.

China's Strategic Emerging Industries: A To-Do List for APT Groups

No sector has gone untouched by intrusions from China-based APT groups. In addition to the frequently publicized data theft from defense companies or government coffers, FireEye has also observed China-based APT groups targeting U.S. firms involved in strategic industries that are not as widely discussed. These industry sectors include electronics, telecommunications, robotics, data services, pharmaceuticals, mobile phone services, satellite communications and imagery, and business application software. In the past year, we have helped many organizations across a broad spectrum of sectors (e.g., business and professional services, finance, media and entertainment, healthcare, and construction and engineering) respond to Chinese APT intrusions.

---

[1] Department of Justice; Office of Public Affairs. "U.S. Charges Five Chinese Military Hackers for Cyber Espionage Against U.S. Corporations and a Labor Organization for Commercial Advantage." May 19, 2014. <http://www.justice.gov/opa/pr/us-charges-five-chinese-military-hackers-cyber-espionage-against-us-corporations-and-labor>

Looking at the current active threats and corresponding data from over ten years of data collection, China-based APT groups consistently target future growth areas for both China and the U.S. These focus areas are described in China's Strategic Emerging Industries initiative, which is a component of the government's 12th Five-Year Plan.[2] The following table displays China's Strategic Emerging Industries and the corresponding number of distinct threat groups we have seen targeting those sectors:

Strategic Emerging Industry (SEI)	No. of China-based APT Groups Targeting this SEI
Clean Energy Technology	3
Next-Generation IT	19
Biotechnology	6
High-End Equipment Manufacturing	22
Alternative Energy	7
New Materials	12
New Energy Vehicles	6

Figure 1: China-based APT groups' targeting of Strategic Emerging Industries

China's Economic Reorientation Will Inform its Future Commercial Cyber Espionage Strategy

China's nearly 20-year period of rapid economic growth has slowed following the global financial crisis, creating significant economic pressures. In response, China has prioritized rapid innovation and focused on stimulating domestic consumption, consumer spending, and services.[3] This reorientation will likely have a dramatic effect on the specific targets China pursues with its commercial cyber espionage program.

Chinese leadership will likely continue to use the theft of intellectual property through cyber means to acquire, mimic, and co-opt innovative foreign technologies. China's efforts to spur innovation will take on even greater urgency if the economy continues to slow and unemployment among college graduates continues to rise.[4] High rates of unemployment among the young and educated could be a destabilizing force in Chinese society, which is not something the Communist Party will tolerate.

Indeed, we're already seeing the targeting implications of China's desire for rapid innovation. This May, FireEye's Mandiant Consultant Services aided Penn State in an investigation of Chinese hackers who had been so deeply embedded in the computer network of its engineering

[2] "State Council 12th Five Year Plan (FYP) on Development of Strategic Emerging Industries." July 2012. <http://www.gov.cn/zwgk/2012-07/20/content_2187770.htm>
[3] "Xi Says China Must Adapt to 'New Normal' of Slower Growth." *Bloomberg*. May 11, 2014. <http://www.bloomberg.com/news/articles/2014-05-11/xi-says-china-must-adapt-to-new-normal-of-slower-growth>
[4] Sharma, Yojana. "What do you do with millions of extra graduates?" *BBC*. July 1, 2014. <http://www.bbc.com/news/business-28062071>

college – which specializes in aerospace engineering, among other disciplines – that the network had to be taken offline.[5] Such an incident is unfortunately not the exception. In the past year alone, we responded to at least two other cyber espionage incidents involving top U.S. schools engaged in sensitive, state-of-the-art R&D.

APT actors will likely continue to target U.S. labs, university research institutions, and small businesses and start-ups – organizations that may lack either the understanding of the risk or the resources with which to secure their technical and scientific research. APT actors may also try to exploit trusted third-party relationships to compromise organizations with better defenses. Given the Chinese leadership's focus on understanding and advancing entrepreneurship, actors may pursue information on the leadership, management, and organizational culture of highly innovative organizations.

Current and Future Trends for Key U.S. Commercial Industries

Environment, Energy, and Agriculture

As its economy has grown, China's environment has been severely degraded, with the demands for energy, land, and materials outstripping available resources. The country recently declared a "war on pollution" to clean the country's choked skies and waterways.[6] Soil pollution has reduced agricultural output, degrading more than 40% of China's arable land and making China more and more heavily reliant on imported food.[7] Securing adequate natural resources, reversing or stemming environmental damage, and enhancing food security are now national priorities.

Consequently, we expect this reality to increasingly drive Chinese APT groups' attempts to pilfer U.S. technology and expertise. Some examples of the APT trends we have observed include the following:

- Environmental damage has dramatically reduced agricultural output in China, transforming food security into a key concern for leadership. It may also be driving cyber espionage activity. Last summer, FireEye saw one Chinese APT group target four different companies involved in farming, agricultural chemical manufacturing, and agricultural equipment manufacturing.

- Reliance on coal for electricity generation is the main culprit of China's poor air quality, resulting in plans to construct 13 new nuclear power plant reactors by 2018.[8] In 2012, shortly after the Chinese government released its nuclear energy safety strategy, FireEye observed one of the most sophisticated Chinese threat groups we track conduct an espionage campaign targeting companies in niche parts of the nuclear industry.

---

[5] Riley, Michael A. "Chinese Hackers Force Penn State to Unplug Engineering Computers." *Bloomberg*. May 15, 2015. <http://www.bloomberg.com/news/articles/2015-05-15/china-hackers-force-penn-state-to-unplug-engineering-computers>

[6] "China to 'declare war' on pollution, premier says." *Reuters*. March 4, 2014. <http://www.reuters.com/article/2014/03/05/us-china-parliament-pollution-idUSBREA2405W20140305>

[7] Patton, Dominique. "More than 40 percent of China's arable land degraded: Xinhua." *Reuters*. November 4, 2014. <http://www.reuters.com/article/2014/11/04/us-china-soil-idUSKBN0IO0Y720141104>

[8] Graham-Harrison, Emma. "China warned over 'insane' plans for new nuclear power plants." *The Guardian*. May 25, 2015. <http://www.theguardian.com/world/2015/may/25/china-nuclear-power-plants-expansion-he-zuoxiu>

- Breakthrough renewable technologies are all but guaranteed to top Beijing's list of technology acquisition priorities. We expect that companies with experience in solar panel and wind power turbine technology (in which Chinese companies already used pilfered technology to undercut foreign competitors)[9] will occur with electric vehicles, emission reduction technologies, battery development, and other energy-saving products. In 2014 FireEye observed a China-based group steal data from a company involved in some of these niche renewable energy technologies.

Future-Oriented Technologies, Surveillance, and Big Data

Manufacturing still remains one of China's key economic drivers, and the Chinese leadership clearly recognizes the potential of next-generation technologies. Our analysts have observed approximately 20 different Chinese APT groups target companies involved in next-generation IT and high-end equipment manufacturing. One instance included the targeting of an electronics organization specializing in law enforcement-related surveillance technologies that probably support the government's push to ensure domestic security and otherwise monitor the populace.

China has set the goal of leading the world in the "Internet of Things," earmarking $800 million for investment by 2015.[10][11] Chinese companies are also making rapid strides in artificial intelligence.[12] Looking forward, we expect to see further attempted data theft of R&D related to the Internet of Things, artificial intelligence and robotics, big data, and 3D printing.

Healthcare and Pharmaceuticals

Facing critical challenges in the public health and pharmaceutical sectors, the Chinese leadership seems again to have turned to cyber espionage. We believe this activity is ultimately geared towards advancing domestic champions, and possibly to prepare firms for foreign ventures and partnerships. China seeks to implement universal healthcare by 2020, and there are definite concerns over rapidly rising healthcare costs.[13] Spending on pharmaceuticals in China is expected to exceed $107 billion in 2015, and China will be the world's second-largest drug market by 2020.[14] A series of demographic shifts leading to an aging population with growing

---

[9] Cardwell, Diane. "Solar Company Seeks Stiff U.S. Tariffs to Deter Chinese Spying." *New York Times*. September 2, 2014. <http://www.nytimes.com/2014/09/02/business/trade-duties-urged-as-new-deterrent-against-cybertheft.html>

[10] Voigt, Kevin. "China looks to lead the Internet of Things." *CNN*. December 3, 2012.
<http://www.cnn.com/2012/11/28/business/china-internet-of-things/>

[11] Ibid.

[12] Zhang Rui. "Baidu CEO proposes national AI project." March 12, 2015.
<http://www.china.org.cn/china/NPC_CPPCC_2015/2015-03/12/content_35030729.htm>

[13] Franck Le Deu, Rajesh Parekh, Fangning Zhang, and Gaobo Zhou. "Health care in China: Entering 'uncharted waters.'" McKinsey. November 2012.
<http://www.mckinsey.com/insights/health_systems_and_services/health_care_in_china_entering_uncharted_wate>

[14] Wang, Shirley S. "A New Cancer Drug, Made in China." *Wall Street Journal*. April 2, 2015.
<http://www.wsj.com/articles/a-new-cancer-drug-made-in-china-1428004715>

obesity, cancer, and hypertension rates only adds urgency to the healthcare problem.[15] [16] [17]

FireEye has observed more than eight Chinese APT groups pursue victims in the pharmaceutical and healthcare industries, successfully targeting business and strategic plans and goals, as well as information from human resources and legal departments. We have seen some APT groups pursue specific, cutting-edge research and intellectual property related to certain critical health challenges. For instance, one APT group has extensively tried to target oncology-focused biotechnology.

Targeting Personal Data

Intellectual property and business information is not the only type of data in which targeted threat groups have shown an interest, although it is by far the most frequently stolen. It appears that advanced cyber threats, some of which may be based in China, have stolen significant amounts of personal data from several different organizations in the past year.

The motivations for stealing this type of information are not yet entirely clear. It is possible that this interest in personally identifiable information and related data is ultimately for monetary gain and criminal purposes, as we know that some threat actors operate as contractors. In fact, we classify at least 3 of the groups we track as operating on a contract-for-hire basis.

Another working hypothesis is that the stolen information could be used for broader espionage purposes, such as to better facilitate follow-on activity by identifying specific individuals, or to make more effective social engineering campaigns.

It is still too early to make a determination, but these developments certainly underscore that the threat landscape is constantly evolving.

Conclusion

China-based cyber espionage actors will likely continue to target U.S. industries in the growth areas that we have described above. Since it is extremely difficult for even security conscious companies to withstand a targeted attack from a nation state, we recommend that companies prepare to respond rapidly to a breach in order to minimize the impact or adverse consequences.

In January 2015, we released an annual threat report that presents insights, statistics, and analysis drawn from the combined experience of our Incident Responders. This year's report portrays a threat landscape that is more complex than ever, with security teams finding it increasingly difficult to prevent, detect, analyze, and respond to advanced attacks. Some highlights from this report include the following:

---

[15] " Ageing China: Changes and challenges." *BBC*. September 20, 2012. <http://www.bbc.com/news/world-asia-19630110>

[16] Pang Li. "Obesity is a growing concern in China.". <http://www.china.org.cn/china/2012-09/14/content_26521029.htm>

[17] French, Paul, "Fat China: how are policymakers tackling obesity." *The Guardian*. February 12, 2015. <http://www.theguardian.com/global-development-professionals-network/2015/feb/12/chinas-body-mass-time-bomb-policymakers-tackling-rising-obesity>

- On a positive note, the time it takes organizations to discover compromises continues to drop. The median number of days attackers were present on a victim's network before being discovered dropped to 205 days in 2014 from 229 in 2013 and 243 in 2012; however, this is still too long and some breaches can go undetected for years. In an extreme case, we identified one organization that had been breached for over eight years without knowing.

- However, it is becoming more and more difficult for organizations to detect breaches on their own. In 2014, only 31 percent of organizations discovered via their own resources that they were breached – down from 33 percent in 2013 and 37 percent in 2012.

- Attackers have also improved their counter-forensics, and as a result, they are more capable of concealing their activities by leaving less evidence behind, posing a challenge for both detection and incident response.

These trends are likely to continue for the foreseeable future, particularly in light of the rapid adoption of mobile and cloud computing technologies, which provide advanced cyber threats with additional attack vectors.

PANEL II QUESTION AND ANSWER

VICE CHAIRMAN SHEA: Thank you very much. Thanks to all our witnesses.

I'll lead off with the first question. Mr. Tiao, you mentioned that President Obama issued an Executive Order in April declaring cyber attacks a national emergency and expressed his authority to impose financial sanctions on foreign hackers.

To your knowledge, has President Obama exercised this authority under that Executive Order?

MR. TIAO: No. To my knowledge, no. I think that the administration's quick announcement that the Thanksgiving 2014 hack of Sony Entertainment was attributable to the North Koreans was significant. It took place before that Executive Order, but it signaled a clear intention of the administration to make public statements and to take public action against nation-state actors.

So I think that really sets the stage for the use of that Executive Order, but I think that with all these types of things and these types of directives and executive orders, it takes time to implement this. There is a process by which the Treasury Department, the Attorney General and other agencies need to work together to actually implement that. So to my knowledge, the answer is no.

VICE CHAIRMAN SHEA: Okay. So he hasn't done--hasn't exercised his authority yet, to our knowledge, since April--since it was issued in April.

I'm going to read something that I found very striking. It's written by the Henry Kissinger Fellow at the Council of Foreign Relations, Robert Blackwill, and Ashley Tellis, and it's a little long so I apologize, but I'm going to ask you to tell me very briefly whether you agree with what they write:

For the past decade, the United States has tolerated incessant cyber attacks by China on the U.S. government, critical infrastructure, and businesses. Virtually nothing has been done to stop this cyber assault. And the name-and-shame approach toward China has clearly failed. The U.S. indictment of five PLA officers, of course, had no impact on China's cyber espionage.

The Department of Defense cyber strategy published in 2011 announced a new doctrine arguing that harmful action within the cyber domain can be met with parallel response in another domain known as the equivalence. No such equivalence has been exacted on China. Such passivity on the part of the United States should end, especially since there is no way to reach a verifiable cyber security agreement with China.

Do you agree with that statement? Each of you?

MR. POINDEXTER: No.

VICE CHAIRMAN SHEA: You don't agree with it?

MR. POINDEXTER: No.

VICE CHAIRMAN SHEA: Why?

MR. POINDEXTER: Well, I read Rob Blackwill's article, too, and I'm sympathetic with a lot of the things he says, but here's the problem you get into in cybersecurity if you start escalation. The Chinese have already given us a warning with those attacks in South Korea and the attack on Sony. I mean how did you interpret that? I interpreted it as saying if you mess with us again, we've got some destructive mechanisms, not just theft of data, but some real destructive mechanisms that we can use. You want to escalate that issue? Go ahead.

VICE CHAIRMAN SHEA: Okay. I'm glad you said that because I'm trying to set up my final question--

MR. POINDEXTER: Okay.

VICE CHAIRMAN SHEA: --which was why we haven't responded? I mean I read your testimony, Mr. Tiao, and it's very good, but you said hopefully some day--the words "some day" leapt off the page--some day the government and private sector will get together and figure out models of deterrence, and then you say there's little analysis devoted to figuring out how to react to this.

My God, it's massive theft, massive damage to our economy, and to our security. The President has called it a major threat to national security.

And the question I had is why? Why have we not responded adequately? And is the answer because we're afraid of blowback, and that the costs that will be exacted from us we're unsure about and therefore we just sort of collapse into tentativeness? Is that--

MR. TIAO: So if I may respond to your first question--

VICE CHAIRMAN SHEA: Sure.

MR. TIAO: --before I try to address your first question? It's my view that the government has taken significant steps. Now in my testimony I talk about deterrence, and I think that there is a lot of room to--there's a lot of room for progress with respect to trying to deter Chinese cyber commercial espionage, but in terms of what the government is doing, there's quite a bit that actually is happening.

The investigative efforts that are designed to identify the actors behind the keyboards, their methods, their technologies, and the tactics--and to share that information with the private sector, that is very, very significant.

The FBI is working closely. The FBI leads a major task force that brings together 20 different agencies that conduct cyber investigations from a military, intelligence, and law enforcement standpoint. And they work closely together, and their ability to work closely together has improved where they are doing coordinated investigative campaigns--

VICE CHAIRMAN SHEA: But--

MR. TIAO: --and network operations. So that's one piece. Sorry.

The diplomatic efforts initiatives of the administration starting in 2012 were brand new and unprecedented. There have been various network defense efforts by DHS, and so I think that there are a lot of things that are happening. I think that there is much more that can be done, and in terms of signaling deterrence, that's an area that really requires a lot of attention. But in terms of efforts to block this activity, more difficult--

VICE CHAIRMAN SHEA: The first part you mentioned is defensive.

MR. TIAO: Right.

VICE CHAIRMAN SHEA: It's defensive. And I agree it's significant; it's defensive. But it's not a cost exaction strategy. You're not exacting costs on the behavior. You're just maybe defending against it more effectively. So is that the game? We're just going to be in years of just sort of defending ourselves, or are we going to actually try to shape the behavior such that this no longer occurs or gets significantly reduced?

MR. TIAO: In my--

VICE CHAIRMAN SHEA: Ms. Weedon, why don't you--I'm sorry.

MS. WEEDON: Oh, no, that's okay. Well, I think that you bring up an important distinction with differentiating between sort of a defensive posture and thinking that you can prevent it versus taking more of a proactive approach, which is sort of acknowledging this is going to happen so how do we then mitigate the risk and mitigate the sort of enormity of impact that happens.

And I think, at least from the private sector perspective, we have seen a shift in companies over the last year or so really talking about this issue at much higher levels, at the board level. We've seen a shift in mind-set in adopting different security programs that take into account this new reality that you really can't prevent this from happening, but rather you could focus on finding the bad guys faster by conducting risk assessments, compromise assessments. We have seen the time to detect a breach go down. Still, last year we crunched the numbers, and the average time that attackers were in an environment was 205 days.

But I think that you're underestimating the enormity of dealing with this. It's not just a technical issue. It's a policy; it's a business process issue. So it's--

VICE CHAIRMAN SHEA: No, I'm talking about U.S. public policy. I agree from a corporate perspective, it's probably very difficult. But the United States is different than the corporations that inhabit--

MS. WEEDON: Uh-huh.

VICE CHAIRMAN SHEA: --the country.

So, anyway, Mr. Tiao, did you have something you wanted to--I cut you off, and I didn't mean to do that.

MR. TIAO: That's quite all right. I think, and maybe I've just been in Washington for too long, but I think that in order to take action against a nation-state like China where we have a complex relationship, a complex economic and security relationship, it's a little more complicated than taking sort of a quick strike action against say the North Koreans with whom we don't have a similarly complicated relationship.

So I think it's easier for the President to announce that it's North Korea that is to blame for the Sony hack and that we're going to take some sort of action; right? It's harder with China, and I think that there is more of a foundation that you need to establish in order to be able to take sort of serious deterrent action, and I think the administration is trying to do that.

Is it doing it as fast as they would like or as the rest of the country would like, I'm sure the answer is no, but I think that things are happening, and that they are moving in that direction, but certainly you couldn't move fast enough to address this problem.

VICE CHAIRMAN SHEA: Okay. Thank you.

Commissioner Wessel.

COMMISSIONER WESSEL: Thank you, all, and Ms. Weedon, I am a big fan of all that your company has done so thank you. Not only a great commercial enterprise, but you've actually also led on a lot of policy issues. So thank you for pushing that debate and for being here.

Mr. Tiao, I'd like to follow up on a number of the questions because we're talking about denial, deterrence, mitigation, and to me mitigation, denial is really a cyber network security issue. Deterrence is a question of when will the Chinese stop, and that's probably when there is a sufficient cost that we tip over.

It seems to me we've hamstrung ourselves in a lot of ways, and it's been a long time since I went to law school so correct me anywhere where I'm wrong here. The five PLA member indictment was a sealed grand jury indictment so under rule 6(e), that information can't be utilized elsewhere. So it was great that Hickton and the government did that, but there's no cost.

You know, in my view those--and as part of the indictment, as I remember, they released the pictures--those people became heroes on China's People magazine for taking the crown jewels out of a number of U.S. entities, and other than not being able to vacation in the U.S.they got off scot-free.

There was a transmission of that data back up to a number of Chinese entities who then presumably used it in the marketplace to their advantage. Moving forward to that advantage, our government has not yet done anything about that. There has not been a sanction.

How would you counsel a private sector entity, any of those five companies, or anyone else who faces a similar action? What kind of relief should you seek? Could you do some kind of civil action? Are there other tools that might be available to you under U.S. law? Would you counsel one of your clients as it relates to, let's say, 8(k) disclosures that if they were informed by the government of a hack of sensitive and valuable information, say two years ago, that they should seek recompense in court?

And in so doing, would they have violated their 8(k) requirements by failing to disclose that in a timely manner? It seems that there are all these issues that are so intertwined, that we're watching as China does this, we're mad as hell, but we're not using the tools, businesses for some reasons are not coming forward, our government is not sharing NSA take data attribution, whatever it is, with the private parties.

So, again, we're hoping that China is going to respond to naming and shaming, and ten years in, they're not responding. A lot of questions there.

MR. TIAO: Okay. Lots of questions. All of them I think are terrific questions, and I think they're questions that we in the private sector and when I was in the government were addressing and trying to address. They're complicated.

I guess to unpack that a bit and to focus on a few of the particular questions that you asked, which could really occupy the rest of the time that we have, I think, but--

COMMISSIONER WESSEL: And several Law Review articles.

[Laughter.]

MR. TIAO: But I'll try to keep this short. So, one, I think the value of the indictment-- it's a public document--right. It's available and it's a speaking indictment. So when I was an AUSA, we had speaking indictments, and then we had just straight up indictments; right? And you write a speaking indictment for a particular purpose; right?

So here I think that the value of the speaking indictment is that it detailed the evidentiary basis that an independent entity, the grand jury, found. And that is valuable not because I think anybody really expects us to get our hands on those individuals and prosecute them here in the United States. I think it's because it provides a stronger evidentiary basis for taking diplomatic action.

My understanding also is that--and I'm not a trade lawyer and I'm not somebody that works in sort of the international trade forums--but my understanding is that there are actions that can be taken based upon the existence of those indictments in a trade forum, and my understanding is that the administration actually is looking at that still.

And so I think that these things do take time. They take more time than we would like. We would all like to be going faster, and maybe the administration could be doing things faster, and I'm not in the administration anymore so I can't speak to that. But I think that there are things that can be done of value, of deterrent value, in this arena based upon that indictment even if you don't actually get hands on those--

COMMISSIONER WESSEL: Let me, and it may be for a second round of questions, but go to the counseling of your clients, if you could.

MR. TIAO: Sure.

COMMISSIONER WESSEL: You know a lot of companies don't want to participate in helping the government bring these cases for fear of what it may result in in terms of 8(k) materiality disclosures, and a lot of other things. Forget about your clients--how would you, in general, approach that issue?

MR. TIAO: I don't think I'm supposed to forget about my clients, but--

[Laughter.]

MR. TIAO: But I'm certainly not here speaking on behalf of my clients.

COMMISSIONER WESSEL: Understood.

MR. TIAO: I'm speaking just based on experience. Look, those issues are complicated, and often they're not so much legal decisions as they are business decisions, and a lot of the questions you raise are really business calculations.

Companies work more proactively, especially the sorts of companies that my firm represents. We work much more proactively with the government than ever before because there are many more programs where the government is actually sharing NSA take. They may not be getting it directly from the NSA, but they're getting it from various parts of the government that are now doing a better job of collecting information and then pushing it out to the private sector.

So I think that is a pretty significant step. I mean five years ago, the government was more focused on protecting its techniques, tactics, procedures, its sources, and then a number of years ago, as really prominently reflected in the 2013 Executive Order, it became a major priority for the government to push information that the intelligence community was collecting and the law enforcement agencies were collecting in a timely fashion out to companies that had been identified as victims. And so--

COMMISSIONER WESSEL: But intrusion sets to try to say here's how you can update your firewalls and everything else. It does not go to the question of how do we actually deter? That's denial. And the question is--and I'll stop and do the next round--how do we deter? How do we actually exact a cost that China knows that it has to stop?

MR. TIAO: I think--

COMMISSIONER WESSEL: We'll do that in a second round. Thank you.

VICE CHAIRMAN SHEA: But think about it. That's a great question. Please. But Commissioner Fiedler.

COMMISSIONER FIEDLER: So while you're thinking about that--

VICE CHAIRMAN SHEA: Right.

[Laughter.]

COMMISSIONER FIEDLER: --I'll give you something else to think about. So let me just ask--I'm a non-lawyer so I'm not restricted in my thinking.

[Laughter.]

COMMISSIONER FIEDLER: Now, I deal with lawyers everyday, as you can tell. Right. Now if you steal something, and I buy it from you knowing it is stolen or I receive it, even if I don't buy it, I have now committed a crime in the United States; have I not?

MR. TIAO: [Nods affirmatively.]

COMMISSIONER FIEDLER: So if CNOOC, if a hacker steals fracking technology and gives it to CNOOC, receives stolen property, CNOOC in our view has committed a crime. CNOOC operates in the United States.

I would propose to you that we establish what I'll call a Foreign Intelligence Cyber Court, and there's a reason that I'm doing that, because I want to affirmatively hack, offensively hack the users of the hacked take. Everybody is talking about the hackers. I don't care about the hackers. I want us to hack the users and determine that they had the technology that was hacked in the United States, and punish them, the buyers, the users, by either barring them from operating in the United States, importing product into the United States, perhaps imposing bank sanctions on them, which have proven internationally now, given the banking community, serious.

I mean if we could even do the North Koreans with banking sanctions effectively, we can do just about anybody else. We're doing the Russians now. Now what you're talking about if you disagree with me is the evidentiary problems one has in making that determination, like innocent until proven guilty. But we sanction people all the time on lesser evidence than I'm proposing.

So I don't think that that is a major obstacle. When I think about a problem that I have with employers in the United States, which is my day job, I don't think about a solution to the problem. I think about creating a bigger problem for them so that the one I have is diminished in their view. In other words, the equation is changed. They haven't been able to put me in a box.

We are fumbling, it seems to me. He raised the question of escalation, and you, surprisingly--I'm not talking about going after their grid, okay, in response to their taking our OPM information. Okay. There's--what's it called--the responding in kind or measured response; right? In this case I'm talking about a targeted response. If, in fact, we talk about tasking where they're talking about their national champions and their policies on this, that and the other thing in their Five-Year Plan, then we target those companies for hacking that are receiving our technology, and we take action against those particular companies that is measured.

If the premise is that if it costs U.S. companies market share or money, we don't do it, we are naked. We are naked. And apparently we are naked in the face of Chinese cyber espionage. I don't see in a practical way why that has to be the case except because of our lack of political will, to target in terms of escalation--one.

The other sort of point I would make is that in the OPM breach, you know, everybody argues we overclassify information in the United States government, and in this case, we apparently underclassified. I mean I can't--I mean I can't fault the Chinese for doing what they did. From an intelligence perspective, you've got to be kidding me. It was brilliant. It was brilliant.

We're foolish enough to put my ten-year history--I'm boring so they didn't get much--but everybody's ten-year history and see boom, boom, boom, and figure out their vulnerabilities to approach. That's pretty smart. That we didn't classify that stuff and have it run on networks that were not connected to the Internet is what the problem is in the first instance, our overdependence on sort of access to the Internet rather than making somebody go to a site where they can get classified access.

So I want to look at this not so much as the China problem but as a U.S. problem on how we deal with what is a reality that is not going away. All right. And that means action on our part and defensive action. Nobody has said to me or anybody has testified that there's anything we can do to absolutely defend our information.

As a matter of fact, the contrary seems to be true. So if we can't defend it and we're unwilling to offensively come up with a gameplan, we're cooked. Am I missing something in this whole dynamic?

MR. TIAO: So I'd be happy to take that.

COMMISSIONER FIEDLER: And what's the problem with the Foreign Intelligence Cyber Court?

MR. TIAO: So I think that the President's April 1, 2015 Executive Order is exactly what you're talking about. I think the whole idea is that you've got companies that have assets in the United States, and they want to be able to use sanctions and to freeze those types of assets.

COMMISSIONER FIEDLER: I was reaching a little farther than the United States with bank sanctions.

MR. TIAO: The example--I thought the example you gave was of a company that had a presence in the United States, that they have assets here.

COMMISSIONER FIEDLER: I mean that's only one example. I would say to you that we'd have to have a farther reach than that. We're not waiting for the terrorists to come to the United States when we do a drone strike in Yemen. Why are we waiting for them, you know, for us to hack only those companies that are operating in the United States? I'd hack everybody else. They'll hack everybody else instead. No, can't have that limitation of the territory of the United States.

MR. TIAO: Sure. And I appreciate that. I think that the value of the Executive Order is just that you have some leverage. You have to look for where do you have leverage? Where can effect deterrence; right? So that is one example. It remains to be seen how often or how quickly or effectively it's going to be used, but it is some new authority and a new process within the government to address it that is, I think, sort of analogous to what you talk about, perhaps in a much narrower setting.

COMMISSIONER FIEDLER: I'm actually talking about a different way of thinking than I am process. I think I'm fundamentally talking about a different way of thinking. We can develop the process if the will is there, and the willingness to take the escalatory risk that he's talking about that is short of them coming back at us in a bad way.

By the way, we got Cartwright, the four-star, when he was a four-star, here to say that if they attacked the grid, it would be the equivalent of a nuclear war. Okay. So we're not talking little stuff here.

MR. TIAO: Right.

COMMISSIONER FIEDLER: Okay. But there's a great distance between the two. Okay. And I'm tired of hearing about process and diplomatic process. Something hardball has got to happen for people to understand that we're serious.

MR. TIAO: So with respect to your hypothetical involving--maybe not a hypothetical, but the sort of the hack back issue, which is where you, I think, started your question. Can we go into that company's network to find out if they have the information, if they're using it, and then to prosecute them or to take some sort of a legal action in a cyber international--

COMMISSIONER FIEDLER: Or extralegal action actually. Yeah.

MR. TIAO: Sure. So I think that our government does actually investigate cases involving hacking, and they do use wiretaps and they do use various investigative methods that are authorized by a court to actually investigate whether or not companies have stolen information, and that sort of information is detailed in the indictment from 2014.

COMMISSIONER FIEDLER: Yeah, but we don't need court authorization to hack them in China.

MR. TIAO: That's right. So I don't want to speak in an open environment about what it is that we do overseas, but, yes--

COMMISSIONER FIEDLER: Neither do I.

MR. TIAO: Okay. So that's sort, there's an understanding that there are a variety of things that we might be doing overseas in networks to collect information about what the bad actors or what adversaries are doing in this area.

I think one of the interesting challenges that we've been trying to address from a policy standpoint is can the private sector hack back against another entity--

COMMISSIONER FIEDLER: Well, I mean--

MR. TIAO: --and sort of go into their network, which would currently be a violation of 18 U.S.C. 1030 criminal law.

COMMISSIONER FIEDLER: Well, I mean but there are all sorts of U.S. subcontractors. She mentioned subcontractors in the Chinese context. Subcontracting is not a, I mean you could have a nonprofit hacking company that was funded by the United States.

MR. TIAO: I think that part of--

VICE CHAIRMAN SHEA: I'm going to have to wrap this up.

MR. TIAO: Sorry.

COMMISSIONER FIEDLER: Yeah. Sorry.

VICE CHAIRMAN SHEA: Yeah. And I know Mr. Poindexter seemed to want to get something, but hold off if you can.

Commissioner Tobin.

COMMISSIONER TOBIN: Thank you, Mr. Chairman.

I want to ask about some of our allies, and, Mr. Tiao, I suspect you have clients who are in Japan or South Korea or Australia. Do you?

MR. TIAO: I have clients that have a presence in various parts of the world that may include some of those countries.

COMMISSIONER TOBIN: And are they facing the same situation or is it almost exclusively focused on the United States? What's your sense on the extent of global hacking?

MR. TIAO: So my understanding is that, and I think that Ms. Weedon's written testimony reflects this, there's an abundance of hacking all over the world. I think that the Chinese government is engaged in cyber commercial espionage against targets all over the world, but there are many other nation-states and criminal hacking organizations all over the world that are hacking companies and governments in every major country around the world.

COMMISSIONER TOBIN: Yeah. I'm not asking about other hackers. I'm asking about the PRC hacking for the same reasons they are hacking us along the industries that she's outlined. Are you aware?

MR. TIAO: Based on reports from companies like CrowdStrike, from Mandiant/FireEye, yes, the answer is yes.

COMMISSIONER TOBIN: Okay.

MR. TIAO: But I think that Ms. Weedon may be best positioned to address that, given her role at--

COMMISSIONER TOBIN: So your clients are largely U.S. clients?

MR. TIAO: Okay. So I don't want to speak specifically about my clients, but I will say that based on my collective experience in the government and in the private sector, I think that this is a challenge all over the world. It's not one that is limited to the United States, and there are so many major companies that are Fortune 100 companies that have a presence all over the world.

COMMISSIONER TOBIN: Right, right.

MR. TIAO: And they face this challenge in their network, in terms of attacks on their networks in the U.S., as well as on their networks around the world.

COMMISSIONER TOBIN: And the reason I'm asking is because it seems to me, much as we do with security issues, that there could be some collaboration and coordination on this.

MR. TIAO: Yes, I think there is an increasing amount of collaboration among some countries in terms of sharing information about cyber threats, cyber indicators. I think that the nature of that collaboration is improving.

I'll give you a couple examples. I mean you can imagine that the sort of collaboration that we have with our Five Eye partners is probably just as good on cyber as it is in other aspects of intelligence. I think that right now law enforcement and investigative agencies, like the FBI and the Secret Service, have people, trained investigators, senior investigators, experienced investigators, that are on the ground in places like Estonia, Ukraine, Romania, working with their counterparts in those countries because it's very hard to extradite somebody to the United States.

It's just as effective, potentially just as effective to have a bad actor, whether it's a Chinese hacker or a criminal hacker or another type of hacker, arrested and prosecuted in Estonia or Romania or another, or the UK, or another country, and so increasingly we see that form of collaboration, which requires a lot of not just information sharing but actually working together.

COMMISSIONER TOBIN: So law enforcement wise, you're--

MR. TIAO: Yes.

COMMISSIONER TOBIN: Okay.

MR. TIAO: And then from a network defense standpoint, I think DHS has been working to reach out to computer emergency response teams around the world, their counterparts around the world, to try to share information more effectively. So there is definitely a global need for it, but as with everything in this area, there's a lot of room for progress.

COMMISSIONER TOBIN: Okay. Ms. Weedon, and then I have a specific additional question for you. Did you want to say anything on that?

MS. WEEDON: Oh, yeah, I was just going to confirm. Absolutely. I mean we've written, actually I have a couple of reports I could pass on to you on specifically your question on China-based actors doing commercial espionage in various parts of the world.

COMMISSIONER TOBIN: Okay.

MS. WEEDON: And, you know, in addition to information sharing among law enforcement agencies in different countries, there are private sector organizations that are conducting information sharing as well. I think you mentioned it has a lot of kinks to be worked out, but it's starting to happen.

COMMISSIONER TOBIN: And the other thing you mentioned, Penn State had to take their computer system offline.

MS. WEEDON: Uh-huh.

COMMISSIONER TOBIN: To what extent is that being done? What's the cost? I don't mean financial cost, but how quickly can they get up again? I'd like some sense of the cost of taking it offline. Is it something that could be done preventatively? Remember back to Y2K? There were fault tolerantsystems. To what extent are other companies or organizations doing that as well as Penn State?

MS. WEEDON: I think that remediation after a breach is something that's a case-by-case basis, and that if a company is either notified that they've had a compromise or they find it on their own, they should work with their security teams and incident responders to define what steps to take.

I think taking the network offline is one way that happens sometimes. But it's certainly not something that should happen automatically every time because frequently responders need time to go in and collect forensic evidence, and if you do something, if you make some sort of stark action, you know, the threat actors may be notified that you're on to them. So it's really a case-by-case basis that companies individually make that decision for themselves.

COMMISSIONER TOBIN: And when they take it offline, how fast are the hackers back on?

MS. WEEDON: I think it depends. We've seen groups that sometimes are not kicked out of the environment even after remediation if they're not caught. Sometimes we've seen companies remediate, and then threat actors come again trying to compromise. It depends on how persistent they are and how valuable that specific target is.

Less sophisticated actors we've seen once they've been kicked out have not been able to get back into the environment, so it's a range.

COMMISSIONER TOBIN: Thank you.

VICE CHAIRMAN SHEA: Commissioner Slane.

COMMISSIONER SLANE: Our job is to make recommendations to Congress, and I'm wondering how you would feel if we recommended that Congress enact legislation giving American companies access to the federal court system to pursue damages when they have been hacked by foreign entities?

COMMISSIONER FIEDLER: Private right of action.

COMMISSIONER SLANE: Yeah, private right.

MR. TIAO: That is something that they could do now. I think that the real challenge is the evidentiary basis for proving that. I think that the sort of work that network security companies like Mandiant and FireEye do is really groundbreaking and important, and there is similar work being done by the FBI. We are so much further along in our ability to establish attribution and to identify individuals and entities that are responsible for this sort of hacking activity than we were five years ago or four years ago that we can now entertain that possibility.

But I think that some of the issues that one of your colleagues--I'm sorry--Commissioner--

COMMISSIONER WESSEL: Wessel.

COMMISSIONER FIEDLER: Wessel.

MR. TIAO: --raised, I mean there are significant business implications that are colored by the legal challenges associated with doing that. And whether there are legal challenges or not, there are significant business implications to taking a proactive stance like that if you want to continue to operate in the Chinese market.

And so I think the general view that I'm sensing that the government needs to be doing more to protect these countries is probably where the locus of the deterrent action really primarily needs to reside.

And so, whether the government--

COMMISSIONER SLANE: Excuse me. Let me--I mean put yourself--I'm a U.S. semiconductor company. I'm not doing business in China. I have some special proprietary technology. The Chinese hack in and they get my technology, and they start utilizing it around the world, maybe even importing it in. And so I don't care about offending them, but I want a private right, and maybe in the legislation we authorize our intelligence communities to cooperate, to overcome some of the evidentiary issues.

You know it's interesting that in China if a state-owned enterprise or a state-controlled enterprise is bidding on a big project, they go to the Chinese government, and the Chinese government hacks into the other competitors and gives them the bid numbers. Okay. Wouldn't it be nice if I'm bidding a project to build a bridge in Dubai, and I go to the NSA and say would you please find out what my competitor in Beijing is bidding? I mean that's what we're up against.

MR. TIAO: Would you like to address that?

[Laughter.]

MR. TIAO: I'd be happy to address it, but I feel like I'm doing all the talking here.

COMMISSIONER FIEDLER: So the question is, is that too great an escalation?

MR. POINDEXTER: Yes. Why not? Why not let the intelligence community participate more with industry, especially when they've been hacked? I mean, first of all, because of policy, we have a lot of restrictions on what the intelligence community is allowed to supply a business, and the intelligence community doesn't want to supply that because they know what the problems are going to be.

First, they're going to have problems with who do you support; right? Do we support BAE? I mean BAE is a big British company. They're in the United States. They get hacked. What do we do then? Do we do the same kind of work? I think you're on the right track, though. I think we need a protocol for how to let the intelligence community help business be successful in the United States.

Why let them hack us and get away with it? When I told my mother I was coming to speak to this group, she said what are you going to speak on? I said the Chinese hacking us, and I thought maybe we should do something about it. She said what? We're not doing anything about it?

[Laughter.]

MR. POINDEXTER: No, we're not. If we had done nuclear deterrence the way we do cyber deterrence, we'd be speaking Russian now.

VICE CHAIRMAN SHEA: There's a sound bite for you.

[Laughter.]

MR. POINDEXTER: I didn't mean for it.

VICE CHAIRMAN SHEA: Okay. I'm going to take the next--are you finished, Commissioner Slane?

COMMISSIONER SLANE: Yes.

VICE CHAIRMAN SHEA: I'm going to take the next question. You were all invited before the OPM hack became public, and I was just reading in the papers--by the way, we did invite, for my colleagues' information, people from the OPM, the White House, DHS, to come and explain what happened, but they were unable, let's say, or perhaps unwilling to do so, at least in an unclassified setting.

But I would just--as experts, I just would like to hear your thoughts on the scope, the scale, the purpose, fallout, of that hack. When you read about it, what was your initial reaction?

Ms. Weedon, why don't we start with you?

MS. WEEDON: My initial reaction was actually not a huge surprise, unfortunately. There's been other similar activity and data theft of similar types of information in the past. So I think, to me, while it's troubling the extent of the information stolen, I think that maybe I'm just hardened because I see all this all day everyday.

VICE CHAIRMAN SHEA: Uh-huh.

MS. WEEDON: But, yeah, that was my impression.

VICE CHAIRMAN SHEA: Okay. Mr. Poindexter.

MR. POINDEXTER: I felt exactly the same way. I said I'm not surprised, but I was not surprised for a little bit different reason. In my book I wrote about hacking security clearance information from the government three years ago. USIS got hacked. KeyPoint Federal got hacked. OPM got hacked. Doesn't that kind of follow? That's over three years.

You have to think that it's going to keep happening until you stop it. We seem to have a belief, and it's an unfounded belief, believe me, that when hackers hack you, you can make them go away. The State Department e-mail system has been hacked for three months, and they have not made them go away. The German parliament has been hacked, and they haven't made them go away because once they get in, they substitute that software, they manipulate the system so that they can get back in.

I mean we did this with a 14-year-old ten years ago where he was getting in from England into our systems in the United States, and we tried to stop him, and we couldn't. Now we say to ourselves why can't we stop him? Because they're smart about how they go about hacking.

Now, if you don't have a deterrence that says you hack us and we're going to do "x," you're going to have problems with this forever because they're not going to stop.

VICE CHAIRMAN SHEA: Mr. Tiao.

MR. TIAO: I have to agree, it's not terribly shocking that this would happen. It's disappointing, and since my information, since I recently have left the federal government, was almost certainly included, it's very dismaying.

VICE CHAIRMAN SHEA: Uh-huh.

MR. TIAO: But not entirely shocking. I mean if you look at all the--there have been so many successful hacks of government institutions as well as major private institutions, it's virtually impossible to stop this for--you're talking about a very determined and persistent actor and a very sophisticated one. So, no, it's not entirely shocking.

VICE CHAIRMAN SHEA: Okay. Compare what happened--you mentioned Sony before. This is all--I just know what I read in the paper. Hacked by North Korea--U.S. government believes is hacked--the e-mail, Sony was hacked by North Korea--a Japanese company with major operations in the United States. Took out e-mails that were internal communica--from the Sony employee--top level Sony employees and exposed them, and this was in retaliation for a movie that Sony had made.

The President of the United States, as I recall, actually made a number of public statements expressing outrage about this and pointing the finger, I believe, at North Korea.

And then my understanding, from what I read in the paper, is that we took some retaliatory action, perhaps took down the Internet in North Korea for a short period of time. Okay.

Now compare that with stealing the personal information of four million federal workers. Excuse me?

COMMISSIONER FIEDLER: And maybe more.

VICE CHAIRMAN SHEA: And maybe more. How would you compare both hacks? Which is more important to the United States? Which act is more heinous? They're both heinous. But which is worse in your estimation? Is there a way--because you know what I'm driving at. We took action against North Korea. We haven't seemed to have taken action yet on the OPM.

You said, Mr. Tiao, at the beginning, it's because we took action against North Korea because we could, because the costs, the blowback against us would be negligible, and so that's sort of what I'm driving at.

But I would appreciate your thoughts on what, how would you compare the two hacks?

MR. TIAO: Apples and oranges.

[Laughter.]

MR. TIAO: I mean the reality is they're both serious types of activities, and so it's hard to assess which is worse. It depends really on your perspective I think.

I think that the ability to establish attribution is a case-by-case analysis, and I think in that instance they were, for various reasons that we don't fully understand because we're not inside of the government, and we don't have access to that type of information, they were able to establish attribution with a high level of confidence very quickly, which is unusual.

And so they were able to take action, and for various reasons, diplomatic and economic reasons, it was the appropriate strategy. We don't really know what action they took or whether, in fact, they took action or whether what you talked about, the sort of North Korean Internet going down, is actually as a result of the government's response or whether it was just an independent action by other actors.

I think that for the Chinese government, our ability to establish attribution again is a case-by-case analysis, and so you just have to look at the facts and then look at the economic and diplomatic implications and then make a considered overall judgment call as to what's the best way to act, and, you know, so far, I think that the administration's response has been to improve the government's ability to support network defense by companies, to bring the indictment against the five PLA actors to engage sort of negotiations at the highest level from the President down to his Cabinet secretaries and his senior advisors and then to take other steps in that nature.

VICE CHAIRMAN SHEA: Thank you.

Mr. Poindexter.

MR. POINDEXTER: Cyber operations are extraterritorial. You can conduct operations from Russia that go through China and attack the United States. You can do the reverse. North Korea can attack from China. Anybody can attack from anywhere because of virtualization of our computer systems. We can move them anywhere we want.

Now, the problem becomes in attribution - not where is the attack coming from, but who is actually conducting the attack? And that's why I was so interested in your question. We need to know who's really attacking us sometimes, and in the Sony case, that's where we really needed to know. Right? Was it North Korea? I don't have any idea. I'm not in the government anymore. I don't want to know. Right?

I think what we're--we're focused on the wrong part of attribution, and we need to focus on the part that says who's really engaging with us, and how are they doing it? I'll give you a simple example. The Russian Business Network. The Russian Business Network was moving because they got identified in Russia--and you know this story better than anybody, right--they got identified in Russia and they needed to move their servers. So they tried to find a place where they could move them to, and they invented another country to go to. Actually I think they went to Italy at first, and we found them there, too.

So where did they go next? They went to China. We haven't seen or heard of the Russian Business Network since. Now why is that? Is it because they don't exist anymore? Is it because they're gone? We don't know. And we'll never find out unless we have the kind of details that the intelligence community can give us on what's going on and who's responsible.

VICE CHAIRMAN SHEA: Okay. Ms. Weedon.

MS. WEEDON: Sure. So without getting into qualifying what's worse, I mean the two main differences between what happened at OPM versus what happened at Sony was the nature of the threat actor. Like was mentioned, it's easier to point fingers at North Korea because there's probably less of a backlash in directly naming and shaming them versus what's happened with

China in the past, and also the nature of the attack I think with Sony because it was, as publicly reported, was a mixture of different types of activity, right. It wasn't just data theft. There was destructive malware. There was psychological operations. There was, you know, it was just sort of a perfect storm of activity, which is just a different type of attack, that I think people found it more difficult to wrap their heads around, and then somehow there were perceptions that it crossed the line that hadn't been crossed before.

So I think the nature of who did it and then what actually happened were what makes these two attacks entirely different and not really able to compare.

VICE CHAIRMAN SHEA: Okay. Thank you.

Mr. Chairman, Chairman Reinsch.

CHAIRMAN REINSCH: I wasn't going to--well, actually Commissioner Tobin asked my favorite question, but I wasn't going to get into this, and then something that several of you said started me thinking.

There seems to be kind of a publicity gap, if you will, in the way countries handle these things, and I'm talking about the country as a victim, not as a perpetrator. I don't think very many countries brag about their hacking, and usually they deny it when they're identified.

But this country is pretty transparent about acknowledging when it has been hacked, and it does that in part for I guess public safety reasons. You want people to know so they can take appropriate action on their own behalf.

I assume, I certainly hope, as Commissioner Fiedler said, that our government is doing the same thing to the Chinese that they're doing to us. I don't know that. But I hope so. But, of course, the Chinese never talk about that. So in public perception, they're invulnerable and we're weak, and their systems work and our systems don't, because we acknowledge what's going on here and they don't acknowledge what's going on there.

Does that matter? Does it make a difference? Does a differential in public perception alter the way these issues play out? Does it put us in a stronger or a weaker position?

MR. TIAO: I guess I'd be happy to just respond quickly to that. I think that there actually have been. The way that the--well, the way that the Chinese government has responded, I think, in part, to the arguments from the United States that it is engaging in hacking is to identify itself as a victim, and so there actually have been a lot of--

CHAIRMAN REINSCH: Oh.

MR. TIAO: --statements by the Chinese government about how it is actually a victim. It's not so much a perpetrator, and that it is--and they have provided reports with detailed statistics.

I think you don't see the sorts of reports by Chinese companies or by the government about the specific hacks and the numbers of personal ident--oh, we have--okay. Sorry. Go ahead.

MS. WEEDON: No, I was going to say actually two weeks ago, a Chinese anti-virus firm released a report on a bunch of campaigns that they outlined affected and breached the networks of Chinese, I think, maritime and navy and military networks. And that's the first time that--it was actually interesting that the report put out by Qihoo actually adopted a lot of the same types of verbiage and presentation that a lot of the reports like FireEye and others put out.

So that very much supports their narrative around being victims themselves, and now they're actually, they're starting to put out reports that show, hey, look, this malware is used to break into our networks. So, yeah, that's changing, I think.

CHAIRMAN REINSCH: So that was the first time.

MS. WEEDON: That we've seen a report put out by a Chinese company, yes. But they definitely have the victim narrative on repeat verbally.

MR. TIAO: But I think that there has--there have been public reports in the last month or so about a campaign in China to try to encourage Chinese residents and citizens to improve their cyber hygiene because of the extent and the widespread extent of identity theft. And so I think that that also supports this view that they perceive themselves and are, in fact, victims of cyber crime, as well.

CHAIRMAN REINSCH: Okay. Thank you.

VICE CHAIRMAN SHEA: Commissioner Wessel.

COMMISSIONER WESSEL: Thank you again.

Commissioner Slane, you and I probably agree on 98 or 99 percent of everything. I'm not yet at the point that you appear to be that we should be like China and go after their commercial secrets and hand them to our U.S. companies. I think that is a critical difference between how China does this and we do it. I'm not saying that there aren't intelligence activities the U.S. may be engaged in or other friendlies against China, but I'm not aware that we're taking Chinese commercial information and giving it to our own companies. That may come and I may support that, but I'm not there yet.

I'd like to go back, though, there's a question of whether there is, in fact, a private right of action, and there is under U.S. law, Section 337 of our trade laws, which would allow you to confiscate at the border products that come in that include purloined IP, et cetera.

It's a little more difficult, though, when you go to trade secrets and other information, which I think was more the issue with the five PLA indictment last year. And, again, Mr. Tiao, also because you served so famously for Mr. Durbin many years ago--a great friend--didn't you?

MR. TIAO: I did.

COMMISSIONER WESSEL: Yes. I find that a badge of honor. I am a huge fan of Dick's, so that's a badge of honor. So counseling a member of the Judiciary Committee, a hypothetical member, we have some issues here again, going back to the materiality, you know, when a company is told by the FBI or FireEye or some private entity that you've been hacked, and if they were to take action--try to take action, first, they're going to mitigate and they're going to deal with cleaning up their networks. If they then found out that there was injury, that's often hard to prove, and under the five PLA, they identified the tasking order, the entities that took it, and the information that was provided back to the SOEs, et cetera.

Do you think that U.S. law is adequate that then those companies that were targeted could seek relief, and what would the relief be in a U.S. court? Would they have to prove damages or is the take enough, meaning--Alcoa was one of the entities. Would they have to show that pricing data was taken over some period of time, and that the Chinese underbid them for that period of time and show what the value was? Or is there a value to that information in and of itself?

Are we putting such a burden on U.S. companies that they're basically saying we don't know how to go after this? We're much better able to do attribution sets. We are better able to determine what has been exfiltrated. But then to look at how that has been deployed to the market, either in IP where you can look at a design that's changed or trade secrets or pricing data, shouldn't we be able to just say, as I think Commissioner Fiedler said with CNOOC or someone else, you go after our companies, and we can prove it, we're going to do something in the market, and we're not going to take all the time to prove it was $2 or $20? We have to do something to stop this action.

I'll start with you and then the other panelists.

MR. TIAO: So I think, and I--I think that there actually is a gap in the law with respect to private right of action to take based on trade secret theft. And I could be wrong about that so--

COMMISSIONER WESSEL: There is. It's IP.

MR. TIAO: Oh.

COMMISSIONER WESSEL: You can prove the trade secrets. I believe there is. You're correct.

MR. TIAO: Okay. And as far as, and as I understand it, there is legislation that has been proposed a number of times in the last several Congresses to address this, and that actually has moved pretty far, and so perhaps you'll be considering that at some point.

But I think that the more you can prove in the way of damages, the more impactful your litigation, whether you're in a pre-trial state or whether you're in trial or whether you're trying to prove damages. And so I think what you've identified is one of the great challenges, is it's to show how the information has been stolen has actually been used and then to place a dollar figure on that.

And I think that that's perhaps why it is that pursuing these types of actions in a trade forum is perhaps a lower burden and perhaps more impactful than pursuing a private right of action where you have to establish damages because I just think it's really hard to prove that up.

COMMISSIONER WESSEL: Would you want as part of this to have some, let's say, immunity clause? You know everyone is being hacked. If the FBI comes to one of your clients, your client comes to you and says, look, the government wants my help in going after the Chinese to bring that case for private right of action, let's say.

And your client then comes to you and says, well, do I have an 8(k) disclosure issue? Am I going to face a shareholder derivative action for not knowing in a timely way, not taking sufficient steps? Aren't we at the point where immunity should be offered --I mean there is certainly malfeasance, but if a company is taking adequate steps, if FireEye is saying do this, and they still get hacked, my view is that there should be some kind of immunity because that's just over and above what any reasonable person would do.

MR. TIAO: So I think that generally when a company is advised by any entity, whether it's FireEye or it's another network security company, or whether it's the FBI or the Secret Service, or an agency in the intelligence community, or DHS, it's advisable for them to actually investigate that information and to figure out whether, in fact, there was a hack, and if so, what the extent of the hack is just because they need to protect themselves.

And then I think that once they do that, then they may determine they do have a disclosure obligation to the SEC and to the public or they may not, depending on whether it's material and what the nature of the investigation sort of determines.

And so, and I think that that is sort of--it's sort of a different perspective on the question that you just raised, the scenario you just raised. I think that increasingly companies are sort of receiving information from the government in part because it's become a higher priority for the--

COMMISSIONER WESSEL: No, no, I agree with that, and what I'm trying to find out is how do we take the caution out of a company, a major Fortune 500 who gets that call, takes all the steps, does mitigation, hires FireEye or somebody else to do whatever is necessary, but then the next question is, by taking some action, are they opening themselves up to this hoard of securities litigation lawyers who seize some crown jewel, they can grab some money, when our real interest should be in stopping China from acting, then at that point we look at some kind of immunity clause to say, hey, you are doing everything you can under the law. You've met that threshold.

MR. TIAO: I think that what we can do to facilitate greater collaboration between the private sector and the government are all things that we should consider, and there are, in fact, as I'm sure you're well aware, there is language on immunity in all the information sharing bills--

COMMISSIONER WESSEL: Right.

MR. TIAO: --that have been proposed. And there is some significant questions about what the extent of that immunity is, and whether it's the right extent, and those bills are pending in Congress, and there's new ones, even though generally the same approach has been adopted in most of those bills broadly speaking.

So I think that we need to be creative about whether, you know, how we try to facilitate that without creating sort of a--I'm not sure "moral hazard" is the right term here, but you don't want to disincentivize companies to actually take the best, the steps that they--

COMMISSIONER WESSEL: Agree.

MR. TIAO: --reasonable steps to protect themselves and, or to--yeah. So I'll leave it at that.

COMMISSIONER WESSEL: Yeah. Thank you.

VICE CHAIRMAN SHEA: I would say one of the things you could do to facilitate greater collaboration between the private sector and the government is to ensure that the information you give to the government is secure.

[Laughter.]

VICE CHAIRMAN SHEA: We have three questions and ten minutes. So I'm going to go with Commissioner Goodwin, then Commissioner Fiedler, and then Commissioner Tobin.

HEARING CO-CHAIR GOODWIN: Thank you, Mr. Chairman.

In preparation for today's hearing, I came across an interesting piece, questioning the need and perhaps usefulness of international law in cybersecurity and cyber space, obviously taking stock of the recent hack of OPM where four million people's personal data was hacked, and also referring to a recent report by the Council on Foreign Relations, which suggested that China had been a victim of cyber exploitations that attacked various governmental agencies and research institutes and where they, of course, pointed fingers back at the United States, suggesting to the author that the depth of these cyber attacks going back and forth suggests an environment in which nations are engaged into a race to drill down to the bottom of every data well they think might be useful for their own purposes on the theory that everybody else is doing it but their allies and adversaries.

And in such an environment, the law seems to be playing a very, very diminished role. Now, obviously, international law does not and will not ever prohibit espionage, but should we concede that international law can do little for this problem of cyber attacks? Does it have a role to play? Perhaps imperfect. And if so, what sort of framework should be established?

MS. WEEDON: So I'm not an international lawyer, but I do know in some work I've done that one of the major stumbling blocks to even having a constructive conversation about how international law could apply to some of these concepts is that there's a fundamental lack of agreement on basic definitions.

So we know that China and Russia have a much more expansive view of information security threats, and they don't use words like cyber, and so having--you know, just have a fundamentally different perspective on threats in this space, and so coming to any sort of consensus and norm setting, in that sense, when you have people with radically opposite perspectives on how to even call this activity, is a challenge.

MR. POINDEXTER: I think in some respects law is too slow in its processes to be able to keep up with cyber. That's one of the difficulties that businesses have. If you look at the case of American Superconductor or Ubiquiti Networks, both of them had cases against the Chinese, which they successfully have prosecuted, but in American Superconductor's case, it took four years to get through the Chinese courts to say that they had jurisdiction over that case.

They now get to bring an action four years later. That's too slow. The technology has changed five times since then, and, in cyber, it changes faster than that.

One of the things that concerns me is the Chinese are going after the basic trust elements of the Internet. They're after our encryption technology. They're after our network information services. Google. Google this past month or in April stopped accepting certificates from the NIC in China. Now, how fast do we react to something like that? We're not going to go to court over that. They're issuing bogus certificates, and they're going through different sub-elements to distribute those.

We can't bring legal action for something like that. Now here's your lawyer. Maybe he can talk to some of those issues, but we're too slow. Our law doesn't allow us to keep up.

MR. TIAO: So I may be a lawyer, but the law is a very complicated thing, and so I'm not--and I'm not an international lawyer. I think that one area where you could have an impact is in trade forums. We're fundamentally talking about a commercial activity and assessment as to what are the fair rules of the game. And it's the United States government's position that espionage is fair game. I think that's everybody's position, and that's reflected in international law because it's not prohibited.

But commercial espionage is a different sort of a thing, and so our government's position has been that we don't steal information and then hand it to companies for their commercial gain. And so--and I think that pursuing economic sanctions through the Executive Order or through broader means. I think that pursuing actions in the World Trade Forum, where they have historically brought actions against companies for engaging in unfair tactics, is an area that is right for development.

And I understand that, it's my understanding that that is an area that is being explored actively, and so perhaps that's one area where you can bring--you've got an existing forum that is well recognized, that is well considered, that has proven to be at least somewhat effective, and where you can impose some leverage and deterrent sort of effect potentially.

But I think that a lot of the international law issues have been more about sort of Internet governance. Should it be in the hands of nation-states as opposed to nonprofit organizations? Who are the stakeholders that should be involved? To what extent should censorship be allowed? And then there's just a host of sort of language issues associated with those principles.

And that I think has been a lot of the focus of so-called international law discussions between various nation-states, and they are sort of a little bit separate from the question of commercial espionage, I think, but again I'm not an international lawyer. So--

HEARING CO-CHAIR GOODWIN: Thank you.

VICE CHAIRMAN SHEA: Okay. Our final question from Commissioner Tobin.

COMMISSIONER TOBIN: Great. My question goesback to what Commissioner Slane spoke about in terms of policy recommendations going forward, and I think I have a very good sense of, from the lawyer's perspective and intelligence perspective, but in our last minute or so, Ms. Weedon, can you take off your business hat and think about the expertise your company has, policy-wise, what can the American government do such that we are providing over time tools that better enable businesses and government to protect themselves?

MS. WEEDON: Sure. So that actually--I'm glad you asked that because it also reminded me that I wanted to make a point earlier about deterrence and sort of raising the cost for the adversary, and so I think the steps that the average American company can take, that the government can help incentivize, can raise the cost for the attacker, and what I mean by that is I think that there's--so the government can do several things, right.

So one is that if the government has-- implements greater flexibility with some of the sort of procurement on getting more advanced technologies and not relying on legacy technologies that are clearly not working. Changing the types of metrics that companies use and internally governments use to assess how successful they are in terms of looking at metrics around detecting a breach or resolving a breach.

COMMISSIONER TOBIN: I see.Say more on that one.

MS. WEEDON: Yeah. So if we get back to the sort of conceptual acknowledgement that prevention is not a viable tactic but rather sort of accepting that something is going to happen, and that what we really should be doing is monitoring, hunting all the time, and figuring out how to root them out faster or at least impede their ability to steal as much stuff, which is in my mind a form a deterrence, right, because you're--

COMMISSIONER TOBIN: Right.

MS. WEEDON: --because you're raising the cost for the attackers. So if you can start to measure metrics around can you find breaches faster, can you resolve them faster, that might be a more useful way rather than, you know, metrics that don't necessarily align with sort of the actual threat reality.

Sharing intelligence is important. It's a challenge, and it's not a panacea, but it's something that the government can promote.

I think also education and finding ways to incentivize universities and getting them to train a workforce that can actually deal with what we're facing because right now I think that we're not properly training people, and that we have a skill shortage so those are some of the policy recommendations that come to mind.

COMMISSIONER TOBIN: Excellent. Thank you.

MS. WEEDON: Sure.

VICE CHAIRMAN SHEA: Well, I want to thank all our witnesses, but before you go and before I pound the gavel, I want to thank the staff of the China Commission--Paul Magnusson, Lauren Gloudeman, Kevin Rosier, Nargiza Salidjanova, Nicole Stroner--for their help in putting together this hearing, and I appreciate your time and testimony, and I think we shed a little bit of light on the subject today. So thank you.

The hearing is adjourned.

MR. TIAO: Thank you.